AUTHOR

CLASS No.

822.91

TITLE

....

....

BOOK No.

3925422

THE SEASHELL

A Play in Three Acts

by

JESS GREGG

LONDON

EVANS BROTHERS LIMITED

To Phyllis Anderson *and* Claire Degener

822 91

*Made and printed in Great Britain
by W. & J. Mackay & Co Ltd, Chatham*

The Seashell

This play was first presented in England by Stephen Mitchell on 12th October 1959 at the King's Theatre, Edinburgh, with the following cast:

LUCILLE (SWART) KITTRIDGE	*Patience Collier*
ALICE (DERST) KITTRIDGE	*Ursula Howells*
MRS. KITTRIDGE	*Sybil Thorndike*
AMY KITTRIDGE	*Heather Sears*
FRANK KITTRIDGE	*Sean Connery*
JANET McCABE	*Patricia English*
MARIETTA BATH	*Hilda Braid*

Directed by HENRY CAPLAN *with décor by* CARL TOMS

The action of the play takes place in the parlour of the KITTRIDGE *house outside a small town in British Columbia. It is summer.*

ACT ONE

SCENE 1	Evening
SCENE 2	Night, a week later

ACT TWO

SCENE 1	Late afternoon, Sunday
SCENE 2	Evening, two weeks later

ACT THREE
Later the same night

Running time of this play, excluding intervals, is approximately one hour and forty-five minutes.

PRODUCTION NOTE

THE SEASHELL was written because I could not forget a house. I had been there but once, and in my childhood, and yet it lingered in my mind far more vividly than houses we had actually occupied. It was a dark, sprawling house, entangled by vine and imperfectly sealed with shutters, nucleus to a dark orchard which graduated into darker forest. Even outdoors, one felt shut off from the world. The nearest neighbour was some miles away and the only sound anywhere was the mourning of pigeons in the mansard turret. My father, looking for a new place to settle the family, called it peaceful; but to me it was like a promise of solitary confinement and I was overjoyed when he decided, yes, it was perhaps *too* peaceful.

If that house has since been called haunted, I am to blame; so often have I, in memory, walked its halls, tested its shadows, examined again its astonishing loneliness. And gradually I began to people this house in my imagination. For all her timidity with strangers, Amy was the first one I knew; then Derst and Swart, and finally, with a sprig of mint or thyme pinned to her sweater, Mrs. Kittridge. Gentle women and content, so used to their isolation, they almost mistook it for happiness.

This house, this indoor world, might well be considered a character in the play—a slightly dowdy and apparently pleasant character who gradually betrays itself as dominant and threatening. I best liked that production of THE SEASHELL which had certain walls of scrim, through which could be dimly seen the constant lurking and listening as lives began to overlap in a world suddenly grown small. It was like the X-ray of a house whose sickness was its occupants.

Let there be no confusion, whoever, of isolation and desolation.

For all their sheltered ways and self-delusion, the Kittridge ladies are not bleak. Affection holds them close; even Swart at her testiest worships Amy. They enjoy games and impromptu parties, make their jokes and know how to laugh. Even though gaiety is often only a cover-up, it is one of the things which has held them together. Certainly their way of life is an unusual one, but let me urge that they not be depicted as eccentrics. It is not their clothes or inflections which make them different, but their point of view. The more normal they seem, the better. Be polite, but very, very firm with actresses with a penchant for eye-rolling or rusty black bombazine from the costume room.

Joshua Logan, the eminent American director, tells of the audience resistance to the love story in one of his early productions. The author kept coining brighter lines about romance, but still the out-of-town audiences remained puzzled by the relationship of the young man and woman. Desperation and a nearing Broadway opening finally forced them to experiment with banality. The bright young man cashed a cliché which the author had been studiously withholding: he told the girl, "I love you". Instantly the audience began to respond. It finally understood the relationship.

In THE SEASHELL no such simple and direct phrase is possible until late in the play. The peculiar challenge to both actress and producer is that Amy blunders into love without recognizing it; and it is not a love which most audiences will be expecting. Having no experience with men or love, she does not correctly identify the avalanche of emotion she feels for her newly-found brother at the end of Act One; but unless the audience is able to identify it as love, Act Two will seem static, enigmatic. The special attention paid to this scene in clarity, invention, and feeling, can pay off richly, as I have seen.

An effect I rather liked in one production was the use of recorded harmonica music between scenes—a continuation, as it were, of the nostalgic, rather wistful songs that Swart is apt to play on her harmonica. This music was again introduced to underscore the Amy-Frank scenes late in the first and second acts, and heightened the mood immeasurably.

Another effective device which needs preparation is the floating down of the feathers at the end of Act One, Scene 1.

Use two bright feathers, about twelve inches long, with much of the lower quill bared away to make them lighter and therefore float down more slowly. (Unpared quills are inclined to dive quickly to the floor before they can be seen.) Place the quills loosely in a shallow box, the top of which is hinged and attached behind and above the stairway arch; the box hangs down with its opening flush against the flat. Attach a cord to the lower edge of the box, run it through a pulley to a convenient point for pulling. On cue the cord is given a tug which opens the box and allows the feathers to be released.

On its original tour, THE SEASHELL played the city where my parents have long lived, and on opening night, they lingered in the foyer, listening for audience reaction to the play. "Well, my dear," a woman they did not know told her companion, "this play is the gospel truth about the Greggs."

I hasten to add that gospel truth about us it certainly is not!

JESS GREGG

N.B. Interleaved producers' copies of this play are available, price 10s. 6d. (postage 7d. extra), *direct from the Publishers only*.

CHARACTERS

In order of appearance

LUCILLE (SWART) KITTRIDGE

ALICE (DERST) KITTRIDGE

MRS. KITTRIDGE

AMY KITTRIDGE

FRANK KITTRIDGE

JANET McCABE

MARIETTA BATH

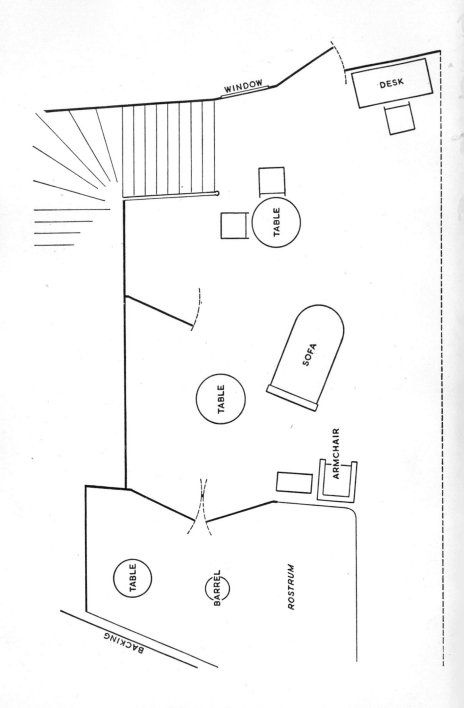

*THE SEASHELL

ACT ONE

Scene i

*The parlour of this house is furnished not wisely, but too well. No parti-
cular era distinguishes the décor; it is an accumulation of several generations.
The walls are papered with some darkening design, over which hangs a
multitude of pictures. The front windows are large but admit little light due
to a heavy growth of vine outside. Off centre, stairs lead to the second floor.
Sliding double doors open on to the dining-room, part of the table being
visible. The front door is on one side of the room, and on the other, a
side door leads to a porch. This, stacked with flower pots and gardening
tools, is backed by a sagging trellis, closely woven with vine.*

> *As the curtain rises, someone is singing in the dining-room. The
> front door opens admitting* Alice Kittridge. Alice, *nicknamed
> "*Derst*", is a sweet, ineffectual woman, child-like, but no longer
> young. As she hastens in, her sister,* Lucille, *peers out of the dining-
> room. Known to her family as "*Swart*",* Lucille *is early in her
> forties. She continually attempts to be funny, perhaps from fear that
> people might be laughing at her anyway.*

Swart (*with relief*). Derst, where've you been?

Derst (*taking off her hat*). I had to work overtime.

Swart. But today of all days. I thought Mr. Parker was letting you
off early.

Derst (*getting her feather duster*). It's my own fault, dear. I rushed over
here during lunch hour to get Frank's room ready. Only I got so
carried away, I was forty-five minutes late back to work, and Mr.
Parker had his gold watch open on the counter.

Swart. I haven't been able to find one thing since I got home. My
blue cook book—did you see it?

Derst (*vaguely*). I put lots of things away—

Swart. Oh-oh. I know what that means. Gone forever.

Mrs. Kittridge (*crossing the porch, calling.*) Open sesame, open
sesame.

(SWART *opens the side door, admitting their mother. Carrying a few garden roses and a basket of green apples, she is a frail, determined woman, whose ingenue manner masks sixty-odd years and the memory of pain.*)

Oh, Derst . . . well, it just looks lovely in here, dear. (*To* SWART.) Hasn't she done a wonderful job of cleaning, Swart?

SWART. Wonderful. I can't find a thing.

MRS. KITTRIDGE. You ought to be getting dressed now anyway, Swart, my darling. The one with the pretty lace collar. I want you to look extra nice for Frank.

SWART (*with a sigh*). Frank, Frank, Frank.

MRS. KITTRIDGE. What's this?

SWART. Nothing, Mama. I'll be ready in time.

MRS. KITTRIDGE. I've been ready ever since noon. Mercy, I've been ready ever since his letter came. Even before. Remember, Derst, I said that morning, I just know today's the day my boy is coming home.

DERST. Yes, Mama, but you've been saying that every day since father stole him away.

MRS. KITTRIDGE. Why, I have not. I purposely wouldn't let myself. Troubles . . . troubles don't afflict so much if you just don't talk about them.

(*The telephone begins to ring. Troubled, all three women look at it without moving. Twice, three times it rings. Then* MRS. KITTRIDGE *sighs.*)

Well . . . let's get on with our work, girls.

DERST. But suppose it's Frank?

SWART. You don't have to whisper. Telephones can't hear you.

DERST. But suppose it's Frank?

MRS. KITTRIDGE. Couldn't be. His bus won't get in till ten past six.

(DERST *puts the flounced hoopskirts of a telephone doll over the phone, as if hiding it might silence it.*)

Now what was I saying?

SWART. That troubles don't afflict if you don't talk about them.

(*The telephone ceases.* AMY KITTRIDGE *enters through the side porch. She is an uncertain, timorous girl, clad in a dark dress more suitable to a middle-aged woman; but she is bare-foot. The pile of junk she carries begins to topple, and her mother runs to her aid.*)

MRS. KITTRIDGE. But . . . why are you bringing all that back in here? I just threw it out.

AMY (*gently*). But, Mama, these are valuable.

MRS. KITTRIDGE (*gingerly inspecting*). Valuable? A single glove?

SWART (*finding a harmonica*). I used to be able to play "Old Folks at Home" on this.

MRS. KITTRIDGE. And this rusty old roller skate. And these feathers?

SWART (*to no one in particular*). "Old folks at home" . . . that's me!

MRS. KITTRIDGE. Nothing remotely valuable here, baby dear.

AMY. Except . . . they were Frank's.

MRS. KITTRIDGE. But he won't want them now. I expect he's grown pretty big.

AMY. But I want him to see we haven't forgotten. That we've kept all his things.

MRS. KITTRIDGE. Well, put them out in the stable then.

AMY. But there's scarcely enough room there even for Klamath. Couldn't I just put them in the stairway closet?

SWART. Now, darling, you want to obey Mama.

MRS. KITTRIDGE (*stroking AMY's hair*). No, no, Swart. Not obey . . . just to please Mama. Because I want that whole terrible closet emptied out, too, all that trash thrown out.

DERST. Now, Mama . . . now, Mama, not my movie magazines.

MRS. KITTRIDGE. But, dear, some of them are a million years old.

DERST. Mama, they're part of my youth!

AMY. Let her keep them, Mama, I'll throw out my stuff instead.

MRS. KITTRIDGE (*reading aloud from one*). "Has Joan Crawford gone Hollywood?"

DERST. I saw her in person once, back when I was working in Hollywood. Anyway, I'm almost certain it was Joan. She came into the shop, and—

MRS. KITTRIDGE. Derst! Now, we just won't discuss that.

DERST. All right, I won't talk about it. But I can't throw out my movie magazines.

SWART. Instead she throws out my best cook book I need this minute.

DERST. Oh, now, sweetheart, you don't need a cook book to fix hot dogs.

AMY. But are we having hot dogs tonight? Again?

SWART (*her idea of a joke*). They won't taste like hot dogs! I'm serving 'em cold!

AMY. Except for Frank's homecoming, we ought to have caviar and roast pig.

SWART. I do the best I can, Amy. I may not have much else to offer, but I give my family the best food in Canada!

AMY. I know, Swart, and I love you, honest, but for Frank, everything's got to be perfect.

DERST. Now, now, now, we really love hot dogs, don't we?
(*And suddenly all three are talking at once.*)

MRS. KITTRIDGE. Girls! (*All three silence.*) If you can't say nice things,
let's not talk at all! What's the matter with us today? This day
. . . I've waited for it nearly twenty years. Surely no one wants
to ruin it for me now.
(*The girls look at each other. Then* AMY *hastens to her pile of
junk.*)

AMY. I'm throwing it right out, Mama.

MRS. KITTRIDGE. Now, wait, now wait. (*She considers.*) Well, all
right then. If it'll keep things happy, we'll hide everyone's precious
junk in the closet. I'll pretend I don't know.

DERST. } Oh, thank you, Mama.
AMY. } You're just wonderful. Did you know that?

MRS. KITTRIDGE. But I'm going to need everyone's help, so please
nothing but happy voices and smiles and singing.
(*Teasingly,* SWART *begins to vocalize. All join in.*)
Now, that's not what I mean, and you know it. Now is Frank's
room all ready?

AMY (*singing*). I've still got to make his bed. (*She starts upstairs.*)

DERST (*singing*). Put a towel out for him, too.

SWART (*singing*). And a wash rag.

MRS. KITTRIDGE (*singing*). And I'll pick some gladiolas.
(*Their impromptu simply convulses them all.* AMY *goes upstairs
and* MRS. KITTRIDGE *goes out the side door.*)

DERST. It does my heart good to see Mama so light-hearted again.
Laughing, smiling.

SWART (*with a sigh*). I just hope she's not in for a terrible disappointment.

DERST. What do you mean? Frank?

SWART. Her and Amy both. They built up this thing in their minds,
till they're halfway expecting a . . . a knight in armour to walk in
that door. An angel from heaven. But we don't know what
Frank'll be like now. He may have even grown up to be like . . .
like Father, God forbid!

DERST. Mustn't speak ill of the dead, dear.

SWART. That man deserted Mama and us and stole Frank! Am I
supposed to praise him?

DERST. Not praise, dear, but . . . forget. Let everyone just forget.

SWART. How are we supposed to forget with Frank coming back into this house? He'll probably open up all those old wounds.

DERST. No, he won't. He'll only be here a few short hours.

SWART. He'll only need a few hours if he's anything like Father. And.—Oh, Derst, I wish he weren't coming home at all.

DERST. Sweetheart!

SWART. I can't help it.

DERST. Why, you used to just love him when he was little!

SWART. Well, I . . . I don't care! It's not fair! I've given my whole life to Mama, and she's never made this much fuss over me.

DERST. Me either, dear. But then, we were never kidnapped from her. (*She discovers a book under a pillow.*) Look! Your cook book! Doesn't that make you feel better?

SWART. Nothing'll make me feel better till he's out of this house.

(*The door has opened and a young man peers in. He is sturdy, intense, in his late twenties; wears sun-tans, a leather jacket, and a cap; carries a duffle bag. DERST stares at him. Seeing her astonishment, SWART turns.*)

DERST. Is it—Frank? Frank Kittridge?

(*He nods. DERST starts toward him, then starts for stairs, then reverses, runs to the side door, calling.*)

DERST. ⎱ Mama, Mama, come quickly. Mama? He's here.
SWART. ⎰ Well—welcome, Frank. I—I'm Swart, if you're wondering.
   And—that's Derst—Mama's out in the garden, you might guess—

DERST (*running halfway upstairs*). Baby dear! Amy. Amy!

SWART. Derst, call Amy.

DERST. I am!

(*MRS. KITTRIDGE hastens in the side door. Startled, unbelieving, she just stares at her son. Then with something like a sob, she runs to him, embraces him. He is ill at ease before so much emotion. At last MRS. KITTRIDGE loosens her arms.*)

MRS. KITTRIDGE. Oh, just let me look at him. He's—he's so big!
   (*She searches his face—suddenly runs her finger up his cheek, looks in astonishment at DERST.*) Whiskers!

SWART. He looks just like Father!

DERST. He does not. He's very handsome.

MRS. KITTRIDGE. Oh, Frank, Frank—where've you been all these terrible years?

FRANK. Well—kind of all over. I was in the navy, and—

MRS. KITTRIDGE. The navy! And I always dreamed you'd be an architect. (*A memory—a little laugh.*) And you said you'd be a burglar, remember? That little suit? (*Laughing to* DERST *and* SWART.) I made him a little suit for his birthday, with short pants, just darling. But he took the scissors and cut them.

FRANK. I had to! Pants didn't have a fly.

MRS. KITTRIDGE. Just ruined that little suit. I said I'd have to tell his father on him, but he said if I did, he wouldn't be an architect, he'd be a burglar. (*She starts to laugh, but it swerves surprisingly into tears. The girls instantly come to her aid.*) Oh, Frank—all the years of you I've missed.

FRANK (*edging away warily*). Don't, Mother.

MRS. KITTRIDGE. Just tears of joy, dear.

DERST. It's just—we weren't expecting you quite this early.

FRANK. I phoned soon as I hit town, but no one answered.

SWART. Oh? I guess we didn't hear it.

MRS. KITTRIDGE. I'm just fine now.

FRANK. Fact is, I phoned twice yesterday to say I'd be getting in early.

SWART. I was kind of surprised you'd look us up at all.

FRANK. Why?

SWART. Oh—what Father probably brought you up to feel about us. (FRANK *turns away impatiently.* DERST, *trying to cover the situation, calls upstairs.*)

DERST (*calling*). Oh, baby dear.

MRS. KITTRIDGE. Let me take your luggage upstairs, dear. Room's all ready.

FRANK. Mother, I wrote I'd just be passing through.

MRS. KITTRIDGE. Oh, we know you wrote it, but—nobody comes to see their family after all these years and then only stays for dinner. You've got to stay for ever.

FRANK. Got to be in Portland on Monday, Mother. Got a job there.

MRS. KITTRIDGE. Get a job here.

FRANK. Except this is more'n a job. Another guy and me—

MRS. KITTRIDGE (*catching hold of his arm*). No, no, darling. Oh, please don't go. Please, darling.

FRANK (*pulling away, calling upstairs*). Hey, Amy? I ever goin' to see you again?

MRS. KITTRIDGE (*calling*). He's home, Amy. Your brother's home! (AMY *edges into view on the stairs.*) Oh, to be able—to be able, at last,

with just a little turn of my head to see all my children together
again!

　　　(*Alternately limp and stiff with self-consciousness,* AMY *starts
　　　downstairs.* FRANK *starts up. She shrinks back.*)

FRANK (*confused*). Amy?

AMY (*in panic, running back upstairs*). I—I forgot something.

FRANK. Yeah. Me!

AMY. Oh, no, I— (*Reappearing, she earnestly, but shyly holds out the
　　　handful of bright coloured quills.*) See? Your feathers. (*Blankly,*
　　　FRANK *examines the feathers.*) It's you who's forgotten.

MRS. KITTRIDGE. You used to stand up on the third floor and drop
　　　them—

FRANK. —down the stairwell. Yes, by God! We had a target.

AMY. We tried to hit a target, a bullseye you drew on some card-
　　　board, and I always won.

FRANK (*simultaneously*). And you couldn't hit a fly. Even when I
　　　guided your hand, you always missed.

　　　(*Both silence simultaneously. Then* AMY *rushes forward, grasps
　　　his hand.*)

AMY. Oh, Frank, it is you!

FRANK (*excitedly*). God Almighty, I can't believe it. Y'know? Even
　　　seeing you grown up, I can't believe it. All of a sudden, it's like I'm
　　　still a kid. Like no time has passed, and I just raced in here from
　　　school.

AMY. You talk so different now.

FRANK. Yeah, maybe because we lived in Nova Scotia.

MRS. KITTRIDGE. Talk to us too, dear, not just Amy.

DERST. We were always wondering where you were. When we
　　　worked the ouija board, Amy'd always ask.

AMY.　　　　　　　⎫ Yes, I always—

MRS. KITTRIDGE. ⎰ And sometimes you'd be in Paris, France. And
　　　once you were even in Shanghai.

AMY. Were you, Frank? In Shanghai?

FRANK. Well—I've been there.

AMY. What's it like? All—Chinese?

FRANK. Kind of Chinese.

MRS. KITTRIDGE. Oh, why couldn't you have let me know where you
　　　were, dear? Why couldn't you have written years ago?

FRANK (*a question he has dreaded*). I—I don't know.

AMY. Did our father make you mad at us?

FRANK. Not at you.

MRS. KITTRIDGE. No. But at me.

FRANK. I— (*He turns from her, quickly busies himself with his duffle.*) Fact is, Amy, he left this package for you. Nothing much, but . . . (*Taking a package from his duffle, he holds it out to* AMY. *She shies from it. He looks at his mother.*) You all still feel pretty strong against Dad, is that it?
> (*A moment of apprehension. Then* MRS. KITTRIDGE *lifts her head proudly.*)

MRS. KITTRIDGE. No. We—we forgave him.
> (SWART *and* DERST *trade a look of relief.*)

AMY. I haven't.

DERST. Oh, now, baby, dear!

FRANK. Why do you say that, Amy?

AMY (*instantly, backing down*). Oh—nothing, I—I probably don't even remember him.

FRANK. Sure you do. Tall as—well, tall as me. And his moustache. We used to watch him shave every morning, remember? (*She shakes her head.*) Sure you do. He was too great to forget.

AMY. If he was so great, why did he want to steal you away from me?

FRANK. Well, I'll tell you.
> (MRS. KITTRIDGE *rises.*)

SWART (*seeing her mother's discomfort*). Never mind, dear! Let's change the subject.

MRS. KITTRIDGE. No, no, it's all right. I—I was just thinking of dinner.

DERST. Mama?

MRS. KITTRIDGE. No, everything's fine, but—I'm sure Frank doesn't want to stand around, talking about a thousand unpleasant old things. He probably wants to get cleaned up from his trip and sit down to a good home-cooked meal, don't you, darling? Well, Swart and I will have it on the table in no time. (*She starts into dining-room, then turns back.*) I'll be running back and forth all the time, stealing a look at my best beau. (*She blows* FRANK *a kiss and goes.*) Come along, Swart, my darling.
> (*But* SWART *lingers self-consciously.*)

SWART. A . . . Frank . . . a . . . I guess we better not talk about it. Father, and all that.

FRANK. Mother said it was okay. She's forgiven him.

SWART. Yes, but—she started to look very tense, and—well, you saw she left the room. We want to shield her from any more pain, don't we? (*She smiles uneasily and goes.*) Hope you brought your appetite. I've got a surprise for you.

AMY (*the moment* SWART *is out of sight*). Now, tell me. Why did our father steal you away from me?

FRANK. He planned on stealing you, too.

AMY. He did? (*Shrinking back.*) I wouldn't have gone. (*Then.*) Why didn't he?

FRANK. When he drove by to pick us up after school, that day, you'd already gone home.

DERST (*glancing at open dining-room door uneasily*). Oh, we don't want to talk about this.

AMY. Oh, please, Derst. I've wondered all my life.

FRANK. He tried coming back for you time after time, but Mama practically had the Mounties out looking for him by then. But up to the end of his life, he kept saying, "When our ship comes in, Frank, we'll go back and rescue Amy".

AMY. You mean kidnap.

FRANK. Well, he said rescue. (*Phone begins to ring. He holds out package.*) Here you go.

AMY (*backing away*). No. You promised you'd give it to me, so you'll just have to stay here till you do.

FRANK. You going to take this present?

DERST (*uneasy about phone*). Well—a . . . dear, take Frank out and introduce him to Klamath.

FRANK. Klamath?

AMY. That's my horse. A man was going to shoot her, but I bought her and nursed her back to life. (*She takes his arm.*) Come on.

FRANK. Somebody going to answer the phone?

DERST. Don't worry. Come along—Frank?

> (*But he has already lifted away the telephone doll and picked up the phone.*)

FRANK. Hello? Which Miss Kittridge? We got three of them. Lucille?

> (SWART *hastens into the room. Her worst suspicion confirmed, she looks in consternation at* DERST.)

She's right here.

SWART. I'm not in. Say I'm not home! (*But he is holding out the*

T.S.—B

phone, and there is nothing to do but take it.) A . . . baby dear, a . . .
weren't you going to show Frank your horse?

AMY. Come on, Frank.

> *(She races out the side door.* FRANK *follows.)*

SWART *(the minute he is outside).* Wrong number. *(And hangs up the phone.)*

FRANK *(turning back).* Hey!

SWART *(uneasily).* It was a wrong number.

FRANK. No, they asked for you. Oh—then that's why I could
never reach you. You don't answer the phone! *(Grinning, he
glances from* SWART *to* DERST.) How come?

SWART *(after an uncertain look at* DERST). It's . . . it's a family matter,
Frank.

FRANK. Well, I'm family. *(But* SWART *has gone into dining-room.)*
What is it?

DERST. Nothing, I tell you.

FRANK. You got creditors, or something?

> *(The word jolts* DERST *terribly. She glances around quickly to
see if anyone has heard.)*

DERST. Shhh.

FRANK. But why's it got to be such a big secret?

DERST. Well, it'd upset Amy to know we're so in debt, and—since
there's nothing she can do to help it—

AMY *(calling from offstage).* Frank?

FRANK. She have a job?

DERST. Oh, Swart and I do. Although my salary isn't— It was
better when I tinted photographs, but now everyone uses colour
film so they put me in the dark room.

FRANK. Yeah, but Amy?

DERST. At least where Swart works, there's someone to talk to. She
works in the sweet shop . . . *(And now there is no evading* FRANK'S
eyes.) oh—Amy? Well—Mama hasn't been too well, and since Amy
really enjoys nursing—

AMY *(running across porch).* Frank?

DERST. Be still, she'll hear!

FRANK. What if she does?

AMY *(entering parlour).* Klamath's even got her eyes open for you.
One of them, anyway.

DERST. Run along, dear. Quickly.

AMY. Oh, must I? Because if Frank's going away again tonight, then
every minute together counts.

FRANK (*touched*). It means a lot to me, too, honey—us being together again.

AMY. Then why do we have to be apart any more?

FRANK. We don't. (AMY's *heart almost stops.*) Why do you think I came back here at all?

AMY. } What . . . what do you—?
DERST. } Do you mean—?

FRANK. Sure. I've had it in the back of my head ever since I was a kid, I guess. That some day I'd come back here again and see you and we'd get to know each other again, have some of the fun we missed.

AMY. Oh, Frank, it's what I dreamed.

FRANK. Always before, I've been half the world away, but this time, coming to this coast of Canada, I said to myself, it's going to be now or never.

AMY. It's what I prayed you'd say. (*To* DERST.) I knew he would. I knew, I knew!

FRANK. Not that it'll be any crystal palace for us either. When we first hit Portland, we may have to rough it a bit.

AMY. What do you mean, Portland?

FRANK. Well, where else would we go?

AMY. Go? (*After a moment.*) But I thought you meant you'd— Oh, Frank, I . . . I couldn't leave.

FRANK. Why not?

(*A pause.* AMY *looks uncertainly at* DERST.)

DERST. She takes care of Mama.

FRANK. I know, but we can iron that out. Maybe you can get a job in Portland, too, and then we'll both send back a little dough.

AMY. Besides there's Klamath. She needs my attention all the time now.

(*Now he studies her carefully.*)

FRANK. I thought you wanted us to be together again so bad.

AMY (*picking up feathers, examining them*). I do.

FRANK. Then what's the trouble?

AMY. We . . . we better get ready for dinner.

FRANK. You got a guy here?

DERST. No, dear, now let's just change the subject.

(MRS. KITTRIDGE *enters with cookies and milk.* SWART *follows.*)

MRS. KITTRIDGE. Brought my beau something to tide him over till dinner.

FRANK (*to* AMY). No, what's the problem?

MRS. KITTRIDGE. Is something wrong? What's happened?

AMY. It's nothing. Honest, Mama.

MRS. KITTRIDGE (*hastening to her, all maternal warmth*). No, I can tell by your voice. I always know.

AMY. I'm fine! (*Tearing loose of her mother, she races out on to the side porch.*)

MRS. KITTRIDGE. Baby dear?

FRANK. What's the matter with her? Something I said?

DERST. Nothing, nothing.

FRANK. I make a simple invitation, and she looks scared to death.

MRS. KITTRIDGE. Now, now, let's not all look so serious. It's such a happy day.

FRANK (*laughing incredulously*). Somebody want to tell me what's going on here?

MRS. KITTRIDGE. Going on?

FRANK. Ever since I got here, you've all been hushing things up or shielding someone.

MRS. KITTRIDGE (*laughing*). No, no.

FRANK. But you do, no kidding. Like not telling Amy you're broke. And the phone—

MRS. KITTRIDGE. Not so loud. (FRANK *tries to continue.*) Dear, she's right outside!

FRANK. That's just what I mean. You're shielding her right now.

MRS. KITTRIDGE. Well, maybe I've had to, dear. Seems the least I can do, after all she's been through.

FRANK. What happened to her?

MRS. KITTRIDGE (*laughing at his density*). Well, dear—excuse me—it seems there was a kidnapping.

FRANK. Me, not her.

MRS. KITTRIDGE. But we never knew when your father would be stealing back for her as well. Day after day, waiting in dread.

DERST. Oh, it was awful, Frank. All those policemen around.

MRS. KITTRIDGE. And believe me, policemen outside the door don't make you feel safe. Only remind you of what you have to fear. That's why I finally begged to have them sent away. We ourselves guarded Amy. Never let her out of our sight.

SWART. Slept in her room at night. And during the day, waited outside her classroom.

MRS. KITTRIDGE. Yes, except—except the school children teased Amy

about that until she got so self-conscious that at last I let her have
a tutor right here at home. A splendid man. A doctor.

DERST. Doc Hawkins.

FRANK. She didn't go to school any more?

MRS. KITTRIDGE. Not much of a life for a girl, was it? That's why
we did everything we could to compensate. Gave her twice as much
love. Shielded her from all our worries. And that's the wonderful
thing, Frank. Out of this shattered home, we . . . we really did
create a beautiful world for her to grow up in. Oh, it wasn't easy,
was it, girls? But when I see the lovely, unspoiled girl today—I
know it's all been worth it.

FRANK (*appalled*). Except—God!

MRS. KITTRIDGE. What say, dear?

FRANK. What—what have you done to her?

SWART. You be still!

MRS. KITTRIDGE. No, no, Swart. He understands. (*But she is uncertain.*)
You understand, don't you, dear? Of course you do. So now we
can just forget the past and enjoy today. Now go wash those
paddies for dinner. (*And she hastens into the dining-room, followed
by* SWART.)

FRANK (*starting to follow*). No, wait—

DERST (*stopping him*). No, dear, please. Oh, don't ruin this happy
homecoming.

FRANK. No wonder Amy won't go with me. You've kept her so
damn sheltered here, she's probably scared to go out of the house!

DERST. No, Frank.

FRANK. Isn't that so? Scared to leave home?

DERST. Just that's she's happier here.

FRANK. How long since she's even gone into town by herself? (DERST
glances away silently.) My God, Derst, she's twenty-three years old!

DERST. No—no, dear. Don't blame—

FRANK. I do blame!

DERST. Then—be sure who to blame! All our lives—even mine—
might be different, if only our father had stood by us.

(*She runs upstairs. Uncertain, and therefore the angrier,* FRANK
goes out the side door. AMY *is sitting in dejection on a bench.*)

FRANK. Come with me, honey. Even for just a week. (*She only
examines the feathers she holds.*) Maybe—maybe our old man did
wrong skipping out that way, but I'll make it up to you now,
if you'll let me. Oh, come along.

(AMY *smiles uneasily, edges away from him.* SWART *slips out of dining-room, listening.*)

Time goes so fast, Amy, and—stuck away here, life could just pass you by, too. You don't want to end up like Derst and Swart—buried alive, and not even knowing it.

AMY. Except, I—Frank, I really am needed here.

FRANK. But I can't leave you here!

AMY. You don't have to leave me. You could stay!

FRANK. Not in a million years. (*Rising, he takes hold of her arm gently.*) Just do what I ask you.

AMY. I . . . I can't.

FRANK. Even—if it means we don't see each other again?

AMY. I—I— (*Suddenly in tears, she runs inside and hastens upstairs.*)

FRANK (*following her inside*). Amy!

(*In the kitchen,* MRS. KITTRIDGE *is singing.* SWART *steps out from the shadows.*)

SWART (*uncomfortably*). A . . . Frank, I asked you not to make any trouble for Mama, and I really must insist—

FRANK (*half under his breath*). Oh, shut up.

SWART. Well! If that's the attitude you're going to take, it'd be better if you left now!

FRANK. Okay with me!

SWART. All right! (*Glances at watch.*) There's a bus that leaves in twenty-five minutes. (*Goes to desk, consults schedule.*) You'll have to wait in New London another hour to make the right connections—

(*A long white feather spirals down the stair-well, followed by a bright red one. Quickly,* FRANK *goes to them, picks them up—looks up the stair-well.*)

—and you won't get into Vancouver till after midnight. You're better off taking the nine o'clock bus like you planned. (*She starts back to dining-room.*) However, do what you want, makes no difference to me. I'll think up some excuse to tell Mama.

(*He looks at the front door, then back to the feathers. After a moment.*)

FRANK. Never mind. I—won't be leaving tonight.

SWART. What? (*He picks up his duffle bag, starts for stairs.*) Staying? For how long?

FRANK. As long as it takes.

SWART. But—your work in Portland.

FRANK (*turning to her. Grimly*). My work's right here!

SWART. And just what do you mean by that?

FRANK. Stick around, Swart! You'll see. (*He goes upstairs calling.*) Amy!

SWART. What do you mean? (*Alarmed now, she runs to the foot of the stairs, calls after him.*) Frank?

THE CURTAIN IS FALLING.

SCENE 2

Night, a week later, MRS. KITTRIDGE and DERST have their hats on. SWART in her bathrobe faces them uneasily.

MRS. KITTRIDGE. But you can't be serious, dear.

DERST. Dear, all he wants is to take us to the movies in town.

SWART. Yes, dear, but ask yourself why?

DERST. To take Amy's mind off her horse passing on.

SWART. Except he began this days before Klamath died. All week he's been working on her.

MRS. KITTRIDGE (*glancing at a newspaper*). Now, Swart, this isn't like you, dear.

SWART. I know it isn't, Mama. And I don't like being disagreeable. I'm supposed to be the sweet shop girl. But—

MRS. KITTRIDGE (*drawing DERST's attention to an advertisement*). Kim Novak.

SWART. —but when I try and say it in an amusing way, you just don't listen! (*She stamps her foot, and they do listen.*) Frank's as much as admitted he's only staying here to get Amy away from us.

MRS. KITTRIDGE. Now why would he want to do a thing like that, dear?

SWART. Well—maybe because—maybe because it's what father wanted to do: steal Amy away to hurt you. So now maybe Frank—

MRS. KITTRIDGE (*laughing*). Oh, sweetheart! Is that why he took a job at the used-car lot in town? To hurt me? Is that why he shares his little salary with us? And fixed the washing machine?

DERST. And fixed my curling iron?

(*A car horn sounds outside.*)

MRS. KITTRIDGE There he is now. Come along, Amy. Frank's here.

AMY (*upstairs*). I can't find my beret.

SWART. Mama—

MRS. KITTRIDGE (*patting SWART's arm*). No, darling. Whatever reason

made Frank stay, just be glad for. Even if it's a cruel reason. It can't
hurt us or change us. But we can change him—with our love.
(*Again the horn sounds and she starts for the door.*)

SWART. All right, Mama, but by then that lovely world we made
here may be gone for ever. And Amy with it!

MRS. KITTRIDGE. Stop saying that!

SWART. You just close your eyes to whatever you don't want to see.
You always have!

MRS. KITTRIDGE. I've been fending off your attacks on Frank all
week, and I just won't have it any more!

SWART. Then why don't you open your eyes and—

MRS. KITTRIDGE. Did you hear me? Be still!

(*A shocked silence.* AMY *comes running down the stairs.*)

AMY. I'm coming, I'm coming.

MRS. KITTRIDGE (*turning from* SWART, *taking off her hat*). Well, you've
just ruined my whole evening! And now I've got a headache.

SWART. ⎱ Well, I can't help it, Mama.
DERST. ⎰ Oh, now, Mama.

MRS. KITTRIDGE. Just ruined everything now, and I'm not going anywhere!

AMY. Oh, Mama, you've got to come. Frank went and rented a car
just to drive us there.

SWART. I didn't mean what I said, Mama.

AMY. Please, Mama. (*But* MRS. KITTRIDGE *hangs up her coat. With
a sigh,* DERST *takes off her hat.*) Isn't anyone going? Derst?

DERST. Oh, we'll do it another time, dear. Don't worry about
anything.

AMY. But Frank'll be just furious if none of us go.

MRS. KITTRIDGE. Then go. I'm not keeping you.

(AMY *wavers then she, too, takes off her hat.*)
No, no, darling. Now I didn't mean to ruin your evening, too.
Just because I'm Ivan the Terrible or whoever it was. Oh, run
along.

AMY. I—didn't much want to go anyway.

(*Outside* FRANK *calls* "Hey, let's go!")
Except—what'll I tell him? He'll be so mad.

MRS. KITTRIDGE. Then let me talk to him, dear. Let Mama handle it
for you. (AMY *hesitates.*) It's liable to be unpleasant, dear. Or . . .
did you want to thresh it out with him? (AMY *does not. She goes
out side door.*) Poor little thing.

(FRANK *enters.*)

Oh, I was just coming out to tell you, dear. I'm afraid our little trip into town has fallen through. Another time.

FRANK (*after scrutinizing them grimly*). Where's Amy?

MRS. KITTRIDGE. Oh, I wouldn't bother poor Amy right now. She's still a wee bit upset. Her horse, you know.

FRANK. Her horse, my ass! Listen—

SWART. Don't you dare say a word like that in front of Mama.

MRS. KITTRIDGE. I didn't even hear it, Swart. But Frank—suppose Amy had?

DERST. What did he say that was wrong?

SWART. You know!

MRS. KITTRIDGE. No, she does not, and neither do you!

FRANK. Okay, okay, I shouldn't have said it. But what I'm trying to say is—

MRS. KITTRIDGE. There, there, I've forgiven you. Now we just won't discuss it.

FRANK. Oh, honest to God! Every time I try to make sense, the conversation gets lost. Last night when I wanted to find out how much money you owe—suddenly, everyone's talking about the best way to break in new shoes!

MRS. KITTRIDGE. But, dear, we had to. Amy was right in the room.

FRANK. I wanted her to be. So she'd get the idea of helping us out by taking a job.

MRS. KITTRIDGE. A job? (FRANK *nods.*) Doesn't it count that she has a job as my companion?

FRANK. But how about a job where she can get some fun out of life, and meet new people and—incidentally, bring in some dough. (*Scoops up a sheaf of letters from desk.*) We got bills! Man, have we got bills!

MRS. KITTRIDGE. Now, now, they'll be paid. My parents left me a very nice annuity.

FRANK. Mama, that annuity doesn't even cover your taxes any more.

MRS. KITTRIDGE. Oh—taxes. Taxes! I'm not going to vote any more if that's all they do!

　　　(*This breaks* FRANK *up. Laughing, he hugs her.*)

You think I'm fooling.

FRANK. So help me, Mama, with you, I can never tell.

MRS. KITTRIDGE (*giggling*). Sometimes I can't myself.

FRANK. But seriously. If Amy could work, and—if we rented one of

the upstairs rooms. The old pink room is never used, and—(Mrs.
Kittridge *giggles again*.)—and the little one in the attic is. . . .
What's so funny now?

Mrs. Kittridge (*laughing*). And every time—every time we want to
use the W.C., there's some strange old man in the bath tub—
                    (Derst *and* Swart *begin to laugh*.)

Frank. No, Mama, please.

Mrs. Kittridge. —scrubbing his back with Swart's toothbrush! Oh,
I couldn't stand it, I'd move out into the orchard.

Frank. It doesn't have to be an old man. Fact is, I've already spoken
to some of the secretaries next to where I work, and—

Swart. You what?

Frank. —two of 'em seemed real interested. Both very nice.

Mrs. Kittridge. I—oh, you make me very proud, Frank. You just
make me so—proud! But—oh, darling—you know what home
means to me. It'd take some real soul-searching before I could ever
see turning my lovely bower into a boarding house. No, I'll need
time on that, dearest.

Frank. If you'll sit down right now, we could figure—

Mrs. Kittridge (*starting for stairs*). But don't worry. We may not be
rich, but there's one thing we do have in this family—not that we
don't have other good things too, but the special thing we have is
the ability to—to— What's the word I want, Derst?

Derst. I don't know, Mama.

Mrs. Kittridge. Well, whatever it is, we certainly have it. All of us.
(*Blowing them a kiss*.) Good night, my dearest dears.

Frank. But, Mama—

Mrs. Kittridge. Swart, will you help me upstairs, I hurt my silly old
foot in the garden today.

Frank. Hey, I'm not finished talking— Mother!

Mrs. Kittridge (*giggling. Continuing on up*). Old man in my bath
tub!

Frank. Mother, don't you give a damn what happens to this family?
        (Mrs. Kittridge *turns on the stairs, looks at him in shocked
        surprise*.)

Swart. Mama . . . ?
        (*But* Mrs. Kittridge *holds up her hand, silencing her*.)

Mrs. Kittridge. I wonder if I haven't given a good deal more than a
"damn" . . . just to have any family at all!

Derst. Now, Mama—

MRS. KITTRIDGE (*retracing her steps downstairs*). Because the only family I had for years was in my dreams. My own parents . . . dead when I was five! Passed around from uncle to aunt. I had to fight to keep that dream of home and family alive. But more than once it has kept me alive. When your father deserted me and stole you, that dream was all I had to hold together what was left of my family!

DERST. He knows, Mama. He didn't mean to—

MRS. KITTRIDGE. My whole life has been fighting for home and family. But not as you fight, my son. Not with anger and accusation. That's what you have to hide, or your home is already destroyed! No! Tenderness, consideration, comfort . . . those are my weapons! That's what has held this family together, knit us tighter and tighter. Like a fist. A fist in the face of the world. Well . . . maybe we haven't won. But we've survived! We've survived! And yet you stand there and say that I . . . that I . . . (*She bursts into tears and starts for the stairs; then turns back, kisses* FRANK *forgivingly.*) It's all right, it's all right. I know you were just teasing Mama. (*She starts upstairs.*) And I was teasing, too. I was as naughty as you. We both ought to be sent to bed without supper. (*And she is gone.*)

SWART. I just hope you're proud, Frank.

FRANK. Okay, okay! Then you try explaining to her.

SWART. She doesn't listen to me any more.

FRANK. Sure she does. You got the head for business in this family. If you'd show Mother the account books— (*She starts upstairs.*) No, wait— (*He catches her wrist, whirling her around. In alarm, she wrests free and thrusts him away.*)

SWART. Don't you dare. (*Then, aghast at herself, almost pleading.*) Oh, Frank—they're all I have in the whole world to care for. I can't let you hurt them. Oh, why don't you leave things be? Why don't you leave us alone? (*Blindly, she stumbles upstairs.*) Why don't you go away?

FRANK (*shouting after her*). Yeah, and maybe I will!

DERST. Don't be cross with her, Frank.

FRANK. God, all I asked was for her to show Mother her account books.

DERST. But that's just it, dear. Those accounts—well—she just pretends to keep them so Mama and Amy won't worry. But actually she knows no more about finance than she does about cooking.

(*Self-consciously,* AMY *enters, side door.*)

Don't let Swart know I told you. She's so sensitive. (*As she goes
upstairs.*) Remember to lock the doors before you come up, dear.
        (*Disregarding* AMY, FRANK *begins to lock up.*)
AMY. You call me? (*He shakes his head.*) Frank, I—I want your honest
advice. Don't you think I should get a new pet right away? (*He
starts for stairs.*) Well, at least say something! (FRANK *turns hotly.*)
No, I know what you're going to say!
FRANK. Why'd you back out tonight? Let me tell you, I'm just about
fed to the teeth!
AMY. I couldn't help it. Mama and them changed their minds,
and—
FRANK. And you couldn't possibly make a decision alone.
AMY. Oh—who wants to do anything alone? It's too lonely.
FRANK. What'n hell do you think you are already?
AMY. Well, not lonely! Well, I'm not! I have many friends. Many!
FRANK. Name three.
AMY (*a beat, and then.*) Mama, and Derst, and—
FRANK. Relatives and animals don't count! (*This so clearly wipes out
everyone, he is abashed.*) Oh, come on. You must have some friends.
AMY (*suddenly*). You know the race track outside New London?
FRANK. And that's how conversations get lost!
AMY. No, because he's a friend, a real one. Doc Hawkins. He's a
horse doctor, see, and taught me everything I know about animals.
And he has this farm near the track that takes care of race-horses
when they're sick or old.
FRANK. Maybe you ought to get a job with this Hawkins.
AMY. Yes, that's what he said—except. Look, your shirt's torn. (*She
takes a threaded needle from a pin-cushion.*)
FRANK. Except what?
AMY. Except your shirt's torn, and that's the job I'm taking. A
seamstress. A French seamstress.
FRANK. Amy, I'm trying to talk seri— Damn it, listen— (*For* AMY
is sewing his shirt with him still in it.) This Hawkins—he's a young
guy?
AMY. No! He's got a son my age. Brucie.
FRANK. He's nice? (AMY *shrugs.*) He's not nice?
AMY. Oh, no! Brucie's very fine. He gave me a dozen apples once.
FRANK. But?
AMY. I—I'm lousy with boys. But I don't care.
FRANK. Amy, you ever been in love?

AMY. No.

FRANK. Ever thought about it?

AMY. Oh, yes. But—men are so treacherous.

FRANK. Now who told you that?

AMY. Everyone I know. Mama said—

FRANK. I can imagine what Mama said. But you should find out for yourself. OW! (*The sewing has got too pointed. He puts an end to it.*) Look—s'pose I introduce you to some guys.

AMY. No! I'm not available to just anyone. I'm not a woman like that.

FRANK. Like what?

AMY. Don't tell me you were in the navy and never heard of women like that? Even I know about them. See, Derst has lots of books hid under her bed—like about La Belle Odessa. Honestly, Frank, she was just terrible. She was very proud though, and the night before she died, to show her contempt for men and their money, she ate a million franc note on a piece of toast! (*Thoughtfully.*) Guess all those noughts gave her wind. (FRANK *laughs. She looks at him in hopeful surprise.*) Am I funny?

FRANK. You're crazy!

AMY. It's because I'm getting to talk exactly like you. That's what Swart says. All the things that used to come into my head to say, that I never said out loud—now I just say 'em!

FRANK. And we lost the conversation again.

AMY (*jubilantly*). A whore! That's what La Belle Odessa was. A whore!

FRANK. Okay, don't overdo it.

AMY. I don't care who hears me! (*But she glances up the stairs, and adds in a whisper, on tiptoe.*) Anyway, I didn't say I approved of such work. Personally, I'd rather starve.

FRANK. No, you can find more suitable work. Like Doc Hawkins—

AMY (*exasperated*). Oh, Frank! Just when we were beginning to have fun! Why do you have to keep harping—

FRANK. Because that's why I stayed. To get you started!

AMY. But I told you. Mama needs me here to take care of her.

FRANK. Oh, come on. It's not Mama who keeps you here!

AMY. It is! That's the truth!

FRANK. The truth? Honey, the day you got the guts to face the truth about this or anything, I'm presenting you with a big silver cup!

AMY. It is the truth! Mama does need me here!

FRANK. The truth is, you're scared to leave home on your own! And you know it!

AMY. Oh, leave me alone! (*The door-bell rings. She runs to the stairs.*) Sometimes I wish you'd never come home!

FRANK. You and me both! You wait right here!

(*But she is gone. The door-bell rings again. With a sigh, he goes to the front door, undoes the two chain-locks, turns the key, yanks open the door. Outside, an easy-tempered brunette, who calls back over her shoulder.*)

MARIETTA. Janet? Come on back. (*To* FRANK.) She thought we'd hit the wrong place.

FRANK. Right place, but the wrong time. I told you tomorrow.

JANET. I know, Frank, but we were out this way anyway, and suddenly couldn't wait to see the place. (*Blonde and good-looking, she enters the parlour.*)

MARIETTA (*following. Looks around in disappointment*). Oh, it's very— charming? Very—very home-like. Isn't it, Jan? Home-like?

JANET. Oh, just exactly like home. Except we have a merry-go-round downstairs and a boa constrictor in the ice box.

MARIETTA. Her father owns the amusement pier over at Port Angeles.

JANET. Owns! He runs the fun house.

MARIETTA (*exasperated*). Could we see the upstairs, Frank?

FRANK. Well—a—I'm afraid—

JANET. Sure, everyone's probably asleep. But—oh, let's take it anyway, Marietta. Sight unseen. It's better than where we are now.

MARIETTA. We ought to look at the beds first.

FRANK. Well, the fact is—a—I'm afraid I jumped the gun in telling you about the room. I been stymied.

JANET.   ⎱ What do you mean?
MARIETTA. ⎰ Stymied how?

FRANK. We're not renting rooms. We're not doing anything! So to hell with it!

JANET. No room?

(FRANK *shakes his head.*)

MARIETTA. Oh—and we had such hopes. We been rooming at Mrs. Fogerty's, and—the bed there— (*Her hand reminds her back of its ache.*)

JANET. You'd think she thought about nothing but bed.

MARIETTA. That's right, dear. Make a good impression. Open that big mouth.

JANET. Am I making a bad impression on you, Frank?

MARIETTA. If plain pineapple juice can make you like this, dear, I want you to promise you'll never even think about beer!

JANET (*to* FRANK). Girls in our office threw a party for Marietta tonight to celebrate her good news.

MARIETTA (*putting some gift boxes on table*). Gave me all these presents.

FRANK. You having a baby?

MARIETTA. Touch wood, for God's sake, not yet!

JANET. She just got engaged.

MARIETTA (*holding out her hand*). Isn't it cunning? (FRANK *examines the ring; has to look close.*) Not as big as Janet's, of course, but then—see, she's marrying our boss. And of course, he's had years longer than my boy to get successful.

JANET. Oh, just years!

MARIETTA. Oh, Janet, I didn't mean. . . . And he's still wonderful looking.

JANET. It's okay. Forget it.

MARIETTA. Mine may be younger, but he's not half the catch. Why for all I know, this may just be a zircon, or—(*Inspecting the ring morbidly.*)—something.

JANET. No, it's lovely! And you're going to be very happy.

MARIETTA (*embracing her*). So are you, don't worry.

JANET. You too, Frank. Okay? (*He nods. She starts for door.*) See you tomorrow.

FRANK. Sure. If I'm still here.

MARIETTA. What do you mean?

(FRANK *shrugs.*)

JANET. No, what do you mean? Are you going away?

FRANK. Yeah, I've had it here.

JANET. But—you can't go yet. I scarcely know you.

MARIETTA. What's that mean?

JANET. That—it's almost easier to say good-bye to old friends than new ones, because—because there's so much yet—that a—a—
    (JANET *keeps trying to say with her hands the word she cannot find. Then, to* FRANK, *with a laugh.*)
I swear it was just plain pineapple juice!

FRANK. But I know what you're trying to say.

MARIETTA. So do I, I'm afraid. (*Pushing* JANET *out the front door.*) Tell the man good-bye.

JANET (*from outside*). We'll miss you, Frank, no kidding.

MARIETTA (*running back for the purse* JANET *has left*). Janet? Your purse! Honestly, that girl! She forgets—(*Snatching up purse, she turns back to door.* FRANK *is so close behind her, she is in his arms. A bit breathless.*) —forgets everything.

   (*Collecting herself,* MARIETTA *hastens out.* FRANK *laughs—then notices she has left her packages on the table.*)

FRANK. Hey! You forgot—

   (FRANK *grabs up the packages, dashes after her, but she is gone. Grinning, he closes the door—suddenly gives a great animal roar.*)

AMY (*upstairs*). What's that? (FRANK *growls again.* AMY *comes running down the stairs in her night-gown.*) Frank? What was that?

FRANK (*but not for her ears*). That was something I been missing.

AMY. What?

FRANK. Nothing you'd know about. (*He crosses to closet, puts packages away.*)

AMY. Are those presents for me?

FRANK (*still angry with her*). No.

AMY. It's my birthday on Sunday.

FRANK. Yeah? Then I better give you this while I can. Catch. (*Throws a package from closet.*) That package from Dad.

AMY. For me? Can I open it now?

FRANK. Why not, since you practically have.

AMY (*holding it up with delight*). A seashell. (*She holds it to her ear.*) You can hear the ocean. Listen? (*She holds shell to* FRANK'S *ear.*)

FRANK. That's a pretty timid sounding sea.

AMY. It's remembering. (*Again, listening to the shell.*) How's it different from the real ocean?

FRANK (*astonished*). Haven't you ever seen the ocean? (AMY *shakes her head.*) But it's only fifty miles off. Well, for God's sake, girl, you ought to! Sure! On your birthday. We could go to the shore on your birthday. (AMY *shakes her head.*) Come on. I could even teach you to swim.

AMY (*still smiling, but backing away*). I don't want to.

FRANK. Swimming's easy! See? (*Extravagantly, he pretends to plunge into the ocean.*) Wow! It's cold! (*He splutters, knocking at his ear.*) Come on in, the water's fine! (*And begins to weave around the room in a frenzied Australian crawl—pauses, looks at* AMY.) Well, come on! (AMY *mounts the sofa and, holding her nose, jumps off.*) Wet, huh? Come on now. Race you to China!

AMY (*dancing around, pretending to swim*). Which way's China?

FRANK. First wave to your right.

AMY. Whoops, I'm drowning. Help, help! (*She swirls about, searching the air with frantic hands. FRANK just stares at her.*) Well, don't just stand there while a girl's drowning. (*He starts swimming after her, but she swirls away.*) Save me, save me.

FRANK. Hold on, I'm coming. Hey! Don't swim so fast!

AMY. Going down for the third time—the fourth—help!

> (*Lurching about, she sinks to her knees. FRANK sinks too, seizing her about the waist. For a moment, they grapple hilariously. But crushed against his body, the frolic suddenly becomes something else to AMY.*)

(*Trying to push him away*). Don't . . . don't.

FRANK. Don't struggle, lady. I got you. Hey, don't struggle.

> (*He lifts her high and her body freezes in exquisite anguish. Then in panic.*)

AMY. Frank, don't! (*She strikes him, and breaks loose of his arms.*)

FRANK. Hey! What's the matter? I hurt you?

AMY. I—nothing. I don't know. (*Then to hide her confusion.*) You're —very strong.

> (*AMY reaches out to touch his biceps then self-consciously hides her hand behind her back. FRANK swells his arm for her. Timidly, AMY puts her hand to it, meeting his eyes with evident admiration. Gently, he puts his hands to her waist and lifts her up again; then slowly sets her down.*)

FRANK. If you'd only trusted me, Amy, I could've saved you easy. Easy!

> (*Speechless, wondering, AMY only looks at him. Then DERST appears on the stairs.*)

DERST. Oh, Frank, the heating pad in my bed has gone funny again. Could you . . .?

FRANK. Sure thing. I'll get a screwdriver. (*He goes into the dining-room.*) And if that don't work, there's always dynamite.

DERST. Isn't he the silly-billy?

AMY. I don't know—I don't know what it was . . .

DERST. What what was?

AMY. We were only playing and—his arms—I nearly—so close—I don't know, I never felt this way before.

> (*FRANK returns.*)

DERST. Here we are. Night-night, baby dear. Sleep tight.

> (*She starts upstairs. FRANK following.*)

AMY. Frank—if—if you still want me—I will.

FRANK. What?

AMY. The ocean. I'll go to the ocean with you.

FRANK (*coming back to her*). You will?

AMY. Would—would that please you?

FRANK. How do I know you won't back out at the last moment, like tonight with the movies?

AMY. But I won't. Not now. Oh, please.

FRANK. Well, thank the Lord! I was just about to give up and clear out!

AMY (*alarmed*). But you won't.

FRANK. Nothing'll get me out of here now! (*He tousles her hair and starts for stairs.*) So that'll be my birthday present to you: the whole damn ocean! And if you like that, you can have the whole damn world!

(*He turns suddenly, leans over the banister.*)

What changed your mind so sudden?

AMY. I don't know. (FRANK *goes upstairs, She sinks down on the sofa, full of something radiant, but not sure what it is.*) I don't know.

THE CURTAIN IS FALLING.

ACT TWO

SCENE 1

Late afternoon, Sunday. MRS. KITTRIDGE *is wrapping birthday presents at the desk.* SWART *is standing on a chair decorating the chandelier with crêpe paper;* DERST *is assisting.* FRANK *races in the side door.* *Outside,* AMY *is calling:* "Not fair, you got a head start!" FRANK *starts upstairs.*

FRANK. Hey there, I get any calls?

DERST. Ask us later, dear, we're in jeopardy.

(FRANK *laughs and is gone.* AMY *rushes in the side door—a very different* AMY *from the timorous shadow of Act One, Scene 1*)

AMY. Frank. (SWART *tries to cover decorations.*) Hey! that looks real pretty.

MRS. KITTRIDGE. It was supposed to have been a surprise.

AMY. Surprise? We always have those up on birthdays.

DERST (*hastening to her*). Tell me, quick. How was the ocean?

AMY. Well—I thought it would be much bigger.

SWART (*with a laugh*). Plenty big enough for people to drown in.

AMY. Not with Frank along. He could save anyone. I hung on to him at first, but after a while— Oh, Mama, I swam alone!

DERST. But tell us how—

MRS. KITTRIDGE. Dear, the birthday party's almost ready, and Amy's got to bathe.

AMY. Bathe? But I've been all day in the water. Beautiful and clear.

SWART. Yes, I've heard about that water, beautiful and clear. They empty sewers in it.

AMY. Oh, Swart! Why are you trying to ruin it for me?

SWART. I was being funny. Besides, we're going to have much more fun tonight than swimming. I made one of my cakes, and got the Mah Jong set ready.

(*The doorbell rings.* DERST *peers out of the window.*)

AMY. Oh, but I can't play Mah Jong tonight.

SWART. But—we always play Mah Jong on birthday nights.

AMY. I know, but—I never liked it much, so tonight Frank's going to teach me to bowl.

SWART. A bowling alley?

AMY. It's all right, everyone bowls nowadays. Frank says I ought to know how, in case I ever go to Portland with him.

SWART. What's this?

AMY. Nothing. Never mind.

(*Giving* SWART's *behind a gentle spank, she runs upstairs.*)

DERST. There's a young woman at the front door. Do you suppose she's here about—you know what?

SWART. Which you know what? We've got so many.

DERST. Are we going to rent rooms after all?

MRS. KITTRIDGE. Answer the door, dear.

DERST. But are we?

MRS. KITTRIDGE. Well, we have such a happy home, why not open our doors and share it with others? (*The girls protest. The doorbell rings again.*) No, no, no, get the room tidied, I can't let it be seen like this.

(*As* DERST *and* SWART *make a dash to clear up the room, the front door inches open and* JANET *peers in.*)

JANET (*calling*). Anyone home? Oh, Frank. (*And now she sees the three women.*) Oh, excuse me.

MRS. KITTRIDGE. But come right in.

JANET (*calling out the door*). Marietta! (*To* MRS. KITTRIDGE.) She's right outside. She snagged her stocking.

MRS. KITTRIDGE. Frank said you wanted to see a lovely room.

MARIETTA (*entering brightly*). Well, here I am, but don't anyone look at my legs.

FRANK (*at top of stairs*). Someone call me?

JANET.   ⎱ Hi, there.
MARIETTA. ⎰ Look who's here.

FRANK (*coming downstairs*). Was beginning to think you'd forgotten. Mama, this is Janet McCabe and Marietta—a—Booth.

MARIETTA. Bath.

FRANK. And my sisters, Derst and Swart.

JANET. Is that German, or what?

MRS. KITTRIDGE. It's really Lucille and Alice. But when Frank was a baby, I thought it'd be nice if he called them Dearest and Sweetheart.

FRANK. Only it came out Derst and Swart.

MRS. KITTRIDGE. Take them upstairs, darling. They want to see the room.

(FRANK *and* JANET *start upstairs.*)

MARIETTA. See you girls later. I wouldn't dream of leaving those two alone. (*She follows them upstairs just as fast as a tight skirt will allow.*)

DERST. Mama?

MRS. KITTRIDGE. No! They're really very sweet.

SWART. Why are you doing this, Mama?

MRS. KITTRIDGE. I—I've been planning on it for a long time.

SWART. Because Frank's making you!

DERST. Is he, Mama?

MRS. KITTRIDGE. No! Never! He merely suggested— (SWART *turns away impatiently.*) Well, I can't help it! If I don't make some concession, he'll go away.

SWART. He'll go away anyhow, Mama. When he gets everything he wants from you, he'll go.

MRS. KITTRIDGE. No! He won't leave me again. He's come home to me for good!

SWART. And unless you stop him, he'll take Amy with him!

MRS. KITTRIDGE. Swart, I told you once before—

SWART. Yes! And I had no proof then. But I do now. Amy's already talking about going to Portland. You heard her yourself!

MRS. KITTRIDGE (*for the first time uneasy*). But—I'm sure that's not what she meant—is it?

SWART. The seashore was just the first step. And next the bowling alley! And after that, probably Portland, where she'll never be able to take care of herself, and we'll worry to death.

MRS. KITTRIDGE. No, he—he wouldn't—he—

SWART. As soon as he gets Amy to go, he'll go!

(*For once,* MRS. KITTRIDGE *hears the truth and it makes her despair. No quick excuse or solution comes to her, and uncertainly she looks about—then heads for the side door.*)

Where are you going?

MRS. KITTRIDGE. Out to my garden. I need to think. (*And she hastens out.*)

DERST. Oh, sweetheart, you just mustn't!

SWART. She's let Frank go too far this time! I can't stand much more. I tell you, I'd leave home—if I had any other place to go. I'm serious! I am! Oh, I know—you think of me as being—witty and—lots of fun—

DERST (*astonished by such a claim*). No, I don't.

SWART. Yes, you do, everyone does! But I'm not! I'm not! If the truth were known, I don't even have a sense of humour.

DERST (*deeply sympathetic*). I know, dear.

SWART. But I make myself say those funny things because—I have to offer something that people want. But there are times when I can't go on being witty. Like now when I see what's happening to our home!

DERST. Maybe if we could make some money quick, Frank wouldn't make us rent rooms. I saw an article. . . . (*Picking up a magazine, she leafs through it.*)

SWART. And Amy—the way she's changing.

DERST. All you have to do is count the bubbles in the picture and send in a letter saying why you like it, and the first prize is just tons of money.

SWART. What bubbles?

DERST. This bubble-bath contest. In the magazine, see?

> (*She holds out magazine. SWART glances at it, begins to get excited.*)

SWART. Entries have to be in by August first—(*Impatiently hands back magazine to DERST.*)—five years ago!

AMY (*coming downstairs*). Who're those people up there with Frank?

DERST. Don't you worry, dear. It's nothing.

AMY. Oh, honestly! I get so tired of never knowing anything.

SWART. No, it's all right, darling. Go take your bath.

AMY (*calling upstairs*). Frank.

SWART. Why do you have to call him?

AMY. Because he tells me when I ask! (*Calling again.*) Frank!

FRANK (*coming on to stairs. To JANET, offstage*). Be right back.

AMY. What's happening that they won't tell?

FRANK (*coming downstairs*). Someone take over with Janet and Marietta?

DERST. I—I've got dinner to look after.

SWART. No, I'm the cook in this family!

> (*She hastens to the kitchen. DERST starts upstairs, but so slowly that FRANK must urge her along with judicious tickling. Then he turns back to AMY.*)

FRANK. What's happening is, I told Mama I'd have to leave if we couldn't rent rooms. It's that important.

AMY. That important? (*FRANK nods.*) Are we—are we poor?

FRANK. We're kind of puny.

AMY (*uneasily*). What'll happen to us?

FRANK. Why, nothing, if we start doing something about it. Getting jobs and all those things we talked about at the beach today. Savvy?

AMY. I savvy everything except—strangers living here with us. Frank, I just dry up with strangers.

FRANK. Honey, you make even the littlest effort, and they won't be strangers.

AMY. But—but—I wouldn't even know how to begin.

FRANK. You know how to smile, don't you? (*She smiles at him.*) There it is! And gorgeous too!

AMY (*dazzled*). It is?

> (*The sound of voices upstairs, and* AMY *hastens away.*)

FRANK. Can't you try, honey? Just for me?

> (DERST, JANET *and* MARIETTA *are coming down.*)

DERST. This lady flies down to Seattle, Washington, every Friday. On business! I think that's just—I don't know what!

FRANK (*indicating* AMY). And this is my sister, Amy. Miss McCabe and Miss Booth.

MARIETTA. ⎱ Bath.
JANET. ⎰ Hello, Amy.

> (AMY *starts to shrink back. Then with a glance at* FRANK, *she crosses to* JANET *resolutely holding out her hand.*)

AMY. I'm very, very, very glad to meet you. (*Looks to* FRANK *for approval. He nods, smiling. Encouraged, she turns to* MARIETTA.) Both. (*They smile.*) A—we saw the ocean today.

JANET. I wish I had.

AMY. You really ought to, some time.

FRANK. She has, honey. She comes from Port Angeles.

DERST (*electrified*). Los Angeles!

FRANK. Port Angeles.

DERST (*oblivious*). I've been there! Hollywood, anyway, and that's almost the same!

FRANK. Port!

DERST. Ever see anyone there? I mean—movie stars?

FRANK (*rapping on the desk with droll exasperation*). This desk—this desk here—we could move it up to your room in case you ever bring your work home.

SWART (*suddenly appearing out of the dining-room*). Move the desk upstairs?

MARIETTA. No, I'm sure that wouldn't be necessary.

FRANK (*to* AMY). See, they both have terrific jobs with the cement brick people.

SWART. Because I do all my accounts at the desk there! (*And she returns to the dining-room.*)

MARIETTA (*covering a pause in the conversation*). A—it's really not that terrific a job. Is it, Jan?

ANET. No. Just plain old stenography.

FRANK. But you love it, don't you? The independence and freedom a job gives you.

> (JANET *looks at him in astonishment. Standing behind* AMY, FRANK *nods vigorously.*)

JANET. Oh—yes. Yes, I love it.

MARIETTA. Yeah, it's grand.

FRANK. Hear that, Amy? Amy's thinking of getting a job, herself.

DERST. What?

AMY. Well, why not? Frank says—

DERST. But I'm glad, dear. Because if you have a job, too, then maybe Frank won't make us rent rooms. (*She freezes. Then apologetically to* JANET.) A—Los Angeles must be lovely this time of year. All that—orange juice.

> (*She hazards a glance at* FRANK. *His look is piercing. She looks around for a quick way out of the room but every escape seems blocked. In panic, she blunders on to the side porch.*)

I think I hear Mama calling.

> (*For a moment everyone gapes. Then suddenly* AMY, *too, darts on to the porch.*)

AMY. Derst, wait.

FRANK. Hey! (*But she is gone. He turns to* JANET *and* MARIETTA *in dismay.*) I—I'm afraid things look a little strained today.

MARIETTA (*with a glassy smile*). No, no, no, no.

FRANK. They'll be okay once they're used to you being here.

JANET. Will they?

MARIETTA. Frank, before we go—

FRANK (*to* JANET). Honest, they'll be crazy about you.

JANET. I'm beginning to know something about you.

FRANK.   ⎱ Like what?
MARIETTA. ⎰ Frank, before we—

JANET. Like—why you waste your time here at a used-car lot instead of—you know. Portland. The boats.

MARIETTA. What boats is this?

FRANK (*to* JANET). And what's the answer?

JANET. Because of Amy.

MARIETTA. You do this day after day! Leave me out of the conversation.

FRANK. No, we don't.

MARIETTA. You do! Talk to each other in some kind of—shorthand! Boats, she says, and sure, he understands. But I don't!

JANET. Because it's something we talked about yesterday.

MARIETTA (*astonished*). We did?

FRANK. Janet and I did. We had a drink together after work.

MARIETTA (*nodding grimly*). Uh-huh!

JANET. And talked about boats! That's his big love. He had this chance to go into business building boats in Portland.

FRANK. Only I'd rather stay here and rent that gorgeous room to you girls.

MARIETTA. I see. (*With a glance at* JANET.) Except—I think you'd better count me out, Frank. And Janet, too.

FRANK. Aw, come on, Marietta.

MARIETTA. Even if we were welcome here—which we're not—it wouldn't be a good idea. I think you know why.

FRANK. My folks, you mean? Them being so . . . different?

MARIETTA. No, that's not what I mean! But since you mention it—

JANET (*interrupting*). Oh, you're great!

MARIETTA. He said it, not me.

JANET. I'm sorry, Frank.

FRANK. It's okay. I know what they are. (*Self-consciously.*) You must think I'm unrealistic as them, even hoping to rent a room here. But I got to.

JANET. So Amy can meet new people and come out of her shell a bit?

FRANK. She's almost out of that shell already! Just a little more, and she'll be free.

MARIETTA. Sure, Frank, and we'd love to help out, but we don't have that kind of time. We're having to run the whole office till Mr. Haley gets home. And then when he does, we'll be planning the wedding. (*Catching* JANET'S *eye, she nods toward door.*) We'd better go.

JANET. But wait—

MARIETTA. For what? This is none of your business!

JANET. Okay, but it won't hurt to discuss it with him.

MARIETTA. And gradually let him talk you into living here, if I know you. The world's biggest pushover for a sad story!

FRANK. Aw, give us a try, Marietta. We're not so bad here.

MARIETTA. Listen, Frank baby, I've got nothing against you. But Janet's the best friend I ever had. (JANET *moans impatiently*.) Jerk though she us! She's made the match of a lifetime, and I can't let her mess it up without putting in my two cents.

JANET. How's this going to mess it up?

MARIETTA. I'll tell you when we get home!

JANET. You can tell me right here!

MARIETTA. Okay. How do you think it'll look to Mr. Haley when he gets back in town and finds you moved in here—alone—talking about boats night and day with a guy who's got all his hair? You know damn well what he'd think. And what everyone in town would think! Why do you want to take chances at an important time like now? Wake up and start thinking of yourself, or honest to God, Janet, you'll wind up right back where you started—(*Angrily,* JANET *turns away*.)—taking tickets at the fun house!

(JANET *turns back, frowning, but thoughtful.* AMY *comes flying in from the porch*.)

AMY. Derst is coming right in. She's eager to tell you— (*But* DERST *still stands indecisively on the porch*.) Derst?

JANET (*slowly*). Never mind, Amy.

AMY. But she really didn't mean that the way it sounded. Why, we'd be ever so pleased to have you live here.

JANET. Thank you, but—

AMY. And you'd be pleased, too, because we have a wonderful view. You can see right through the forest from my room. But— (*A great sacrifice.*)—but if you like, you could have my room.

JANET. That's very generous of you, Amy, but—

AMY. Oh, but I want you to. You don't even have to share your bathroom, because we have three bathrooms.

FRANK. Amy, will you hold it a second?

AMY. Have I gone too far? (*To* JANET *apologetically*.) Swart says I overdo everything.

FRANK. Miss McCabe's trying to tell you they won't be living here.
(AMY *looks at* JANET *in surprise*.)

JANET. I'm sorry.

AMY. Well . . . well, I don't blame you. I wouldn't want to live here either if I were you. We were all so rude, it just makes my ears burn.

But . . . I ask you to believe me . . . usually we are very nice.

JANET (*touched*). I—I can see you are, Amy. (*Suddenly turning on* MARIETTA.) Oh, honestly, Marietta, you're out of your mind!

MARIETTA. Have it your way, honey. (*She opens the front door.*) Back to the fun house. (*And goes.*)

JANET (*to* AMY). Look—even though I won't be living here—what are you doing for lunch tomorrow?

AMY. Why—having it in the garden with Mama, like always.

JANET. Why not come into town and eat with me? At the Lunch Wagon. Food's nothing special, but it'll give us a chance to talk.

AMY (*astonished*). Why . . . why, I . . .

JANET. I mean, if you're going to be looking for a job—well—maybe I could give you some pointers on shorthand, and how to dress, and all that.

AMY (*dazzled*). Why . . . thank you. And you must come over here often, too. I could give you some pointers on— Well, all I know is horses' anatomy, but . . . *any* time! I'm always home. Except tonight I'm going bowling. It's my birthday, you see.

JANET. Why, Amy! Many happy returns.

AMY. Same to you.

JANET (*going to front door*). And I'll see you tomorrow noon. Okay?

AMY. Yes. I mean . . . okay!

FRANK (*following* JANET *out*). I'll see you to your car.

(*They go.* SWART *comes out of dining-room as* AMY *jubilantly starts upstairs.*)

AMY. Wasn't she lovely? And her hair! Just like spun gold!

SWART. Now, darling, you had no right apologizing for us that way.

AMY. Well, sweetheart, someone had to. You didn't even try.

DERST (*entering*). No, no, it's Amy's birthday. Let's all just forgive and forget.

AMY. We didn't make either of those girls feel welcome, and . . . why, they would have paid us for the pleasure of living here.

DERST. Well, dear, money isn't everything.

AMY. No, but it certainly helps when you're poor.

SWART. We are not poor!

AMY. Well, we're puny!

DERST (*shying from these ugly words*). Now, baby dear—

AMY. No, it's all right, Derst. We don't have to be afraid of it. People should learn to face these things, and then they don't have to be so afraid.

SWART. And guess who's been talking to you.

AMY. Well, he's never been wrong yet.

SWART (*with a sigh*). Amy, you're just too trusting.

DERST. Now, let's not call names.

SWART. I'm only saying it for her own protection, Derst. If you remember, we were all so trusting of Father, too. And what happened? He left us in the lurch for some woman.

AMY. Oh, why do you always have to bring up my father?

SWART. Only so you won't think Frank is infallible. Why you saw for yourself how that McCabe girl wrapped him around her little finger.

AMY. Because he wanted to rent her the room so bad.

SWART (*laughing*). Of course he'd like to have her living here. So convenient.

AMY. What do you mean by that?

SWART. Even that loud brunette wouldn't leave them alone together.

AMY. Why, he wouldn't even look at her!

SWART. Look at her? Oh, Amy, you just make me scream with laughter! He followed her outside, didn't he? He's still out there, laughing and fussing with her.

AMY. You be still!

> (SWART *looks at her in astonishment; then, with a little cry, she scurries into the dining-room.*)

DERST. Oh, Amy! You . . . you honestly should go apologize.

AMY. I will not! Libelling Frank that way. Narrow-minded old—
(*But even in anger, she cannot say it.*)

DERST. Old maid? (*She laughs.*) As far as that goes, dear, I'm single, too.

AMY (*covering her faux pas*). Yes, but you're not really an old maid, because you never wanted to get married anyway.

DERST. Yes, I did.

AMY. Swart never loved anyone, she doesn't understand a man like Frank.

DERST. That time I ran off to Hollywood.

AMY. Not that anything she says could touch Frank.

DERST. He was a painter. Oh, a house painter, but—he took me to a Vienna restaurant. Twice! (*Taking* AMY's *hands, drawing her attention.*) Only this bleached blonde waitress—

AMY. I don't care about blonde waitresses.

DERST. Well, he did. That's what men want, I guess—girls with bleached hair.

AMY. No, they don't.

DERST. But, dear, they do! Look at Frank and that Janet McCabe!
     (*Uneasily,* AMY *looks out the front door again.*)
 Is she still there?

AMY (*calling*). Oh, Frank. The party's almost ready.

DERST (*joining her at door*). He doesn't even listen.

AMY. Yes, he does. (*Calling.*) Frank! Better come in now. Frank!

DERST. Well—we don't care. We'll go in to dinner without him.

AMY. No. I'm not hungry.

DERST. But it's your party!

AMY (*calling*). Frank!
     (MRS. KITTRIDGE *comes in the side door with a flowering potted
     plant.*)

DERST. After all the work we've gone to, fixing a nice— Mama, she
     won't eat dinner.
     (MRS. KITTRIDGE *glances sharply at* AMY, *then gives the plant
     to* DERST.)

MRS. KITTRIDGE (*quietly*). Put it in the kitchen. (DERST *goes.* MRS.
     KITTRIDGE *goes to* AMY.) Baby dear— (AMY *turns back to the open
     door.*) Now, Amy, listen to Mama!
     (AMY *shakes her head.* MRS. KITTRIDGE *changes her tack.*)
 Won't you go into the birthday party on Mama's arm? (AMY
 does not seem to hear.) It'd be a help to me, a real help. I hurt my
 silly old foot in the garden.

AMY. You always hurt your foot when someone won't co-operate.

MRS. KITTRIDGE (*now wholly at a loss*). Amy, what's happening?
     What's happening to you?

AMY. Nothing! (*She looks out door again.*)

MRS. KITTRIDGE. Yes! It is! Something's been happening to you all
     week! You're changing into a stranger I don't even know. Grow-
     ing away from us, turning against us. What is it? What is it?

AMY (*turning*). Oh, Mama, I'm afraid.

MRS. KITTRIDGE (*holding open her arms*). Then come back here where
     you're safe.

AMY. But it's not me I'm afraid for.

MRS. KITTRIDGE. Who, then? (*Suddenly* AMY *comes to her arms.*) Tell
     Mama.

AMY. There's . . . oh, there's so much could take Frank away.

MRS. KITTRIDGE. Yes. I know. (*Smoothing* AMY'S *hair, striving for
     poise.*) I do know. So much to tempt him away. I wake up at

night, fearing, fearing, praying: Oh God, don't give him back to
me after all these years and then let him stray off again so soon.
Show me how to keep him content here a little longer. Anything.
Anything he wants, if I can just have us all together under this roof.
But how long can I, with Swart opposing it on one side . . . and
you on the other?

AMY. Me?

MRS. KITTRIDGE. Yes. You. So afraid we'll lose him . . . but you
throw him right into the arms of temptation!

AMY. Mama, I don't!

MRS. KITTRIDGE. Encouraging him to wander off. These trips to the
beach. Pipe dreams about Portland. You can't expect him to want
to stay here when you don't!

AMY. That isn't what I meant when I said—

MRS. KITTRIDGE. Whatever you meant, it'll end up with him getting
dissatisfied with us. Is that what you want?

AMY. No!

MRS. KITTRIDGE. Then for mercy's sake, child, work with me, not
against me! Draw his attention back home. Make him want to
stay home.

AMY. I—I don't know how.

MRS. KITTRIDGE. Why, by showing him he can have twice as much
fun right here. Tonight for instance—we'll make the dinner party
the merriest in the world—laugh till we cry! And afterwards, when
we play Mah Jong—let him win, incidentally—

AMY. Oh, Mama, Frank wouldn't want to play Mah Jong. And
besides, I already promised I'd go bowling with him tonight.

MRS. KITTRIDGE (*closing up*). Very well. Then you'll just have to go
on being afraid for him. (*She starts to go.*)

AMY. But what can I do? If I say I'd rather stay home tonight, he'll
just get mad at me and go bowling with—with someone else.

MRS. KITTRIDGE. Then find an excuse for staying home that he can't
get mad at!

AMY. But that sounds so dishonest.

MRS. KITTRIDGE. When it's for those you love, nothing is dishonest.
          (AMY *turns away rebelliously.* MRS. KITTRIDGE *sighs and goes
     towards dining-room.*)
Well, do what you want. Go bowling, or whatever! But don't
come crying to me when he finally runs out on us, same as his
father did. (*And she goes.*)

AMY. Don't say that!

    (*A sound of whistling has preceded* FRANK, *and now he enters, and races for stairs.*)

Where are you going?

FRANK. Gotta shave. Janet says I'm bristly as a pirate.

AMY. Frank, wait! (*And for once he waits.*) A—I been trying to think how I could repay you for teaching me to swim today. So tonight. I'm going to teach you my very favourite game: Mah Jong!

FRANK. Mah Jong?

AMY. It's terribly exciting. A game of chance, only it's Chinese.

FRANK. And sit on our backsides all night, when we could be bowling? Not me! We want action! (*Hastening upstairs.*) I got to shave, case we meet someone there.

AMY (*calling after him*). Case you meet who there? Her?

    (FRANK *does not answer.* AMY *turns fiercely and kicks the sofa. It hurts. Then, more thoughtfully, she kicks it again—and experiments with a limp. Suddenly, she looks around at the stairs.*)

SWART. Ding-dong bell, everyone. (*Comes into the room.*) Dinner's ready. Come along, birthday girl. (*She turns out the parlour lights, and goes.*)

AMY. Yes.

    (*Only the light from the dining-room door illuminates the parlour.* DERST, SWART, *and* MRS. KITTRIDGE, *offstage, begin singing* "Happy Birthday to You". *Tensely,* AMY *climbs midway up the stairs, then turns.*)

But please, God . . . don't let it really hurt.

    (*Now she backs up a step. Then another. Then yet another, looking down the stairs in dread. Then she jumps forward, grasping the banister midway to propel her forward and into the room. She rolls on to the floor, upsetting a chair. She groans.*)

SWART (*from dining-room*). What's that?

AMY (*dragging herself back up the stairs*). Frank . . . Frank . . . my foot. Frank. . . .

THE CURTAIN FALLS.

SCENE 2

    Evening, two weeks later. FRANK *is on the phone, toying with the telephone doll. Outside, on the porch,* SWART *in her bathrobe, is softly playing the harmonica:* "Old Folks at Home".

FRANK. Sure. Put on my coat and I'm ready. Two minutes is all we need. Okay? Great. See you. (*He hangs up, restores the telephone doll, and shouts up the stairs.*) Hey, Amy. Amy?

> (*He takes his jacket from the hook as* DERST *enters in a Japanese kimono.*)

DERST. Oh, wearing a necktie!

FRANK. So am I. Green striped with pink.

DERST. It is not. It's dark blue.

FRANK (*calling*). Amy. (DERST *is moving a chair up to the table.*) I wouldn't bother moving the furniture tonight.

DERST. But Amy said to. So we can all—

FRANK. —play games. Drop the hanky or pin the tail on the donkey —every night these two bloody weeks since Amy fell downstairs. Honey, I need a vacation!

DERST. What do you—Are you going out somewhere?

FRANK. Hey—why not come with us? Belle of the ball. (DERST *giggles, but waves him away.*) Hey, what's the matter? Don't you like to have fun?

> (*Outside on the porch,* SWART *rises, starts inside.*)

DERST. Oh, more than anything. More than just anything. I used to be just a demon for high life and excitement. Once I actually—

> (SWART, *passing, contributes a sour note on the harmonica and a side-long glance, and continues on up the stairs.*)

Well—never mind.

FRANK. No, go on.

DERST. I've forgotten. Besides, I'm not supposed to talk about it.

FRANK. I won't tell anyone. Come on.

DERST. Well . . . a few years after you were stolen, I went down to Hollywood. It wasn't that I wanted to be a picture star myself, I just wanted to be near them. So I decided to be a movie usher or work in the box office. Oh, Mama just put her foot down, but I was rash in those days. So first I went to the famous Grauman's Chinese Theatre. Well, they already had a girl in the box office there. Hair all bleached and her eyebrows shaved off. That's the kind they wanted. Everywhere I went, that's the kind they took, because that's what men like. Even at the Vienna restaurant. I could have probably got along very well out there, gotten married and everything, if I'd blondined my hair, but I couldn't. I got afraid of what Mama would say. And besides, I'm not that

kind! Ruthless! And that's how you've got to be in this man's
world.

FRANK. Aw, honey—hog-wash! You know better'n that.

DERST (*encouraged*). Well, sometimes I almost think if I ever try
again—

(*A ghostly moan from upstairs startles her.*)

What's that?

FRANK (*calling*). Amy!

AMY (*upstairs, offstage*). I wasn't listening. Anyway, I've heard about
that woman with no eyebrows ten million times.

DERST (*calling up indignantly*). Well, maybe it's funny to you, but that's
how you got to be! (*She starts for dining-room.*) Ruthless!

FRANK. But what were you going to say? If you ever try again?

DERST. Oh, Frank, I've forgotten all that. I'm content now. Don't
make me think.

(AMY *hastens downstairs in a tattered wilting tarlton rose costume.
Her ankle is taped and she limps.*)

AMY. I didn't mean to hurt your feelings. (*Embracing* DERST.) I won't
let you be unhappy. No one can be. I just passed a new law.

DERST. Why, it's your old May Day costume!

AMY (*showing it off to* FRANK). We're all going to play charades tonight. You know—dress up.

FRANK. Oh, no, we're not.

(AMY *turns to* FRANK *in surprise.*)

We just got an invite to a barn dance.

DERST. In a barn?

FRANK. Well, same thing, the Y.M.C.A. (*Looping his arm through*
DERST'S, *he whirls her around, chanting.*) Swing your partner, that's
the way, we'll push old Derst right in the hay!

DERST (*screaming with delight*). Frank, I'll get dizzy!

FRANK. Got to get dizzy! (*Swinging around to* AMY, *who backs away.*)
C'mon, get dressed. Janet'll be by to pick us up any minute.

DERST. Janet again?

AMY. Oh now, Frankie— (*Fussing with his tie.*) How can we go to
a dance, or anywhere else, when . . . my silly old foot!

FRANK. Your silly old foot's had two weeks to get well.

AMY (*limping away from him*). Besides, I've already made out plans
for tonight. Such fun! Everyone'll get dressed up all crazy, and
then—

T.S.—D

FRANK. You trot out that Mah Jong just once more, and so help me, I'll pow you!

AMY (*backing away*). Oh, you will, will you?

FRANK (*following*). Yes'm. Right in the smoosh!

AMY. You'll have to catch me first. (*Darting around the couch gaily.*) Couldn't catch a flea!

FRANK (*in pursuit*). We'll see about that!

> (AMY *dodges behind the giggling* DERST, *and then streaks away from* FRANK *again. He almost catches her, but she vaults over the sofa.*)

DERST. Amy! Your foot!

> (AMY *resumes limping, but it is too late.* FRANK's *face is grave.*)

FRANK. Yeah. That's what I thought! You been faking that foot all week!

AMY. I haven't either.

FRANK. If your foot's well enough to go hurdling sofas, it's well enough to go dancing.

> (MRS. KITTRIDGE *starts downstairs, wearing a tired beaded evening gown of 1914, with a blue crêpe-paper ribbon across the breast and a little gold paper crown on top of her head.*)

MRS. KITTRIDGE. Here I am, all ready for dress-up night. The Queen of Sheba, or whoever, all done up in her best bib-and-tucker.

> (*The doorbell rings.*)

FRANK. We'll go now, Amy.

MRS. KITTRIDGE. It does my heart good to hear you children enjoy yourselves.

> (*Grimly,* FRANK *goes to the door.*)

AMY. But Frank, listen—we could play cards. Draw Poker. Anything!

MRS. KITTRIDGE (*indicating her crown*). Children, look! Do you like it?

AMY (*frantically, as* FRANK *opens the front door*). I could read aloud to you. (*Grabbing a book.*) You'll love it, Frank. Better than dancing.

MRS. KITTRIDGE (*puzzled*). Children!

FRANK (*firmly, to* AMY). You coming?

AMY. No!

> (*Their eyes meet. Then, grimly,* FRANK *leaves.* AMY *hurls the book to the floor.*)

MRS. KITTRIDGE. Amy!

DERST. Now, now! We just passed a new law, remember?

AMY (*despondently seeking her mother's arms*). Oh, Mama, I don't know what to do next.

MRS. KITTRIDGE. Neither do I. (*To* DERST, *quietly*.) Who was that outside?

AMY. No one!

DERST. Why, Amy, it was Janet McCabe.

AMY. Well, let him do what he wants! I don't care!

DERST. There, there, we can still have a nice party. Swart brought home some bon-bons from the shop and we can play cards and—

MRS. KITTRIDGE. No, when you're upset, I always say there's nothing like the ouija board.

DERST. I always say—

MRS. KITTRIDGE. No, you don't, dear. Now go get the bon-bons.

(DERST *hastens into dining-room*. MRS. KITTRIDGE *gets out the ouija board*.)

Sit down, baby dear.

AMY. I can't. I don't believe in the ouija board.

MRS. KITTRIDGE. I'm not sure I do either, but I remember how it comforted me when your father deserted us.

AMY. Frank's not deserting us!

MRS. KITTRIDGE. I didn't say he was.

AMY. You practically did. Comparing him to his father.

MRS. KITTRIDGE. It's not the same at all. Your father left us for some— (*Suddenly uneasy*.) Never mind.

AMY. Some woman.

MRS. KITTRIDGE. Well, just don't talk about it.

AMY. No, we won't talk about it, we'll just go on hinting and hinting! (MRS. KITTRIDGE *tries to speak, but* AMY *overrides her*.) Why not come right out and admit you're afraid Janet is trying to get him away?

MRS. KITTRIDGE. Don't say that!

AMY. I didn't! It was you!

(*Suddenly both are alarmed*.)

MRS. KITTRIDGE. No! You!

AMY.   ⎫ Not the first time.
MRS. KITTRIDGE. ⎰ Be still, be still!

MRS. KITTRIDGE. Whoever said it. (*Thoughtfully*.) If that should be in his mind—

AMY. What is it?

MRS. KITTRIDGE. People only run away together when it's impossible to be together right where they are. And it's not impossible here. In fact—in fact, it might be the very thing to keep him content, here.

AMY (*in dread*). What do you mean?

MRS. KITTRIDGE. A girl-friend, silly. This Janet McCabe. If we actually encouraged their friendship, drew her more and more into our home.

(AMY *backs away from the suggestion, not knowing how to fight it.*)

Well, dear, if it keeps them here.

(*The front door opens and* FRANK *enters.* AMY *grasps his arms in the wildest job and whirls into the room.*)

AMY. Oh, I knew you'd come back! I knew, I knew!

(JANET *has followed* FRANK *in.* Now AMY *sees her and back away as if from fire.*)

FRANK. We decided you might like some company.

JANET. Why, it's a masquerade! Don't you all look charming!

(DERST *returns with the bon-bons, and seeing* JANET, *promptly circles back to the dining-room, shielding her face.*)

And Miss Kittridge.

DERST (*caught. Lamely*). Oh . . . what a surprise.

JANET. Madame Butterfly?

DERST (*dreadfully conscious of her old kimono*). It . . . used to be pretty, but things fade. (*Unconsciously, her hand has strayed to her cheek.*) I . . . oh, I think I heard Swart calling. (*She darts upstairs.*)

JANET (*somewhat wistfully*). I wish my folks had done things like this. Costume parties and all. We never got together.

MRS. KITTRIDGE (*graciously*). Well, then join us.

(AMY *turns to her mother sharply.* JANET *is looking down at her own dress.*)

Oh, a costume. Here. Here. (*She starts to take off her crown.*) We'll share it.

JANET (*laughing*). No, no, no. You look so pretty.

(FRANK *has snatched up the telephone doll and now puts it on* JANET'*s head.*)

FRANK. Here! (*And with a great bow.*) Welcome to the party, Catherine the Great!

JANET. How do I look, Amy? Pretty gorgeous stuff? (*She sashays across the room.*)

FRANK (*applauding*). Fabulous, kid!

JANET. Where's your costume?

FRANK. Couldn't afford one.

JANET. Wear mine.

(*She tries to fit the doll over his head, and they scuffle hilariously. Outraged,* AMY *snatches the doll away.*)

FRANK. Hey!

AMY. No! Derst made that telephone doll, and I won't let people make fun of it!

FRANK. We weren't making fun of it!

MRS. KITTRIDGE. Now, now, never mind, it's nothing to worry about. Amy's just not feeling well tonight. Her foot.

FRANK (*hotly*). Her foot, my—

MRS. KITTRIDGE. No! That's enough! Now—temper has no place at a party, a masquerade party. We're supposed to laugh and be gay. Now—there's some ginger ale in the ice box, Frank. Yes, pour it in the sherbet glasses and we'll make-believe it's champagne. Go on. (*He glances at* JANET. *She nods. He goes.*) A— can't you run along and help him, Baby?

AMY. No.

MRS. KITTRIDGE (*trying to signal*). He may need help.

AMY. I'm staying right here.

(*An awkward little pause.*)

JANET. I'm afraid our butting in has sort of ruined your party. Maybe we should come back another time.

MRS. KITTRIDGE. But no. No, dear. We love having you here. I was telling Frank only tonight, "Let your family enjoy Janet, too. Who knows . . . she might even enjoy us."

JANET. That's very sweet of you, but—

MRS. KITTRIDGE. Not sweet. Just that I know what it's like for a young girl with no close family ties. Because I had none either. My life didn't really begin till I was married.

AMY (*in anguish*). Mama!

MRS. KITTRIDGE (*turning, all innocence*). Yes, Baby?

AMY. Oh, please don't.

MRS. KITTRIDGE. Don't what, dear?

AMY. She doesn't want to hear about that.

MRS. KITTRIDGE. You don't even know what I was going to say. (*To* JANET.) I think that marriage is—

(AMY *runs to dining-room door, and calls.*)

AMY. Frank? You better get back here. I think Mama's just about to tell how you cut up the little suit.

FRANK (*getting in there, quick*). Hey, Mama, for God's sake!

MRS. KITTRIDGE (*to* AMY). Why, I was not!

FRANK. Can't I trust you alone? The minute my back is turned—

MRS. KITTRIDGE. I wasn't going to say a thing about the little suit.

JANET. Oh, please do.

FRANK (*pouring the ginger ale*). Don't get her started, because from there she'll have to explain how Swart caught whooping cough when she was five. And how marvellous Derst was in the High School health pageant. What was it she played? Good Digestion? And scarcely forgot her lines at all.

MRS. KITTRIDGE. She didn't forget her lines. Never. Never!

FRANK (*passing the ginger ale*). And from there, it's an easy step to the disasters. Oh, she's terribly proud of our disasters.

MRS. KITTRIDGE. Why, I am not. I never even discuss disaster.

FRANK. Never! Never!

MRS. KITTRIDGE. It's not our disasters I'm proud of, but the way we rose above disaster. Knit together, tighter and tighter, like a . . . yes, a fist.

FRANK. } A fist in the face of the world!

MRS. KITTRIDGE. } A fist in the face of—

(*She turns to him astonished; finds herself ridiculous. Suddenly she giggles.*)

Why, you took the words right out of my mouth. (*She laughs again.*) A fist in the face of the world. Imagine it. Tired old lady with red hands and a tinsel crown, a fist in the face of anything. Oh, I must be a sight for you.

(*Suddenly abashed,* FRANK *glances away.*)

No, no, no. Laugh, dearest. It is funny. I think so, too.

JANET. Oh, Mrs. Kittridge, I'm sure he—

MRS. KITTRIDGE. No, it's all right, Miss McCabe. We're always fooling this way. He wasn't laughing at me. With me. He was laughing with me. Because he knew I was only trying to be funny. (*She starts upstairs.*) He's my son. He wouldn't hurt me for the world. (*And laughing again, she turns back.*) Oh, I can hear it now, the way he'll introduce me to his friends. "Meet my mother— otherwise known as 'The Fist'!"

(*She lifts her "champagne glass" to them, and laughing, dis- appears up the stairs.*)

FRANK. God, I thought we were all—I thought everyone was kidding.

JANET. So did I.

FRANK. I—I'd better—(*He signs and goes upstairs.*) Sorry.

JANET. It's all right. (*Turning to* AMY, *who has drawn back, her head bowed.*) Run on up, honey, I'll be okay.

AMY. No, I—(*Then with resolve.*) I stayed here on purpose, because I—I wanted to talk to you.

JANET. Wonderful. Here.
> (*She sits down on the sofa, pats a cushion, indicating for* AMY *to sit down beside her.*)

How've you been lately, stranger?
> (AMY *remains standing however, her courage suddenly gone. A brief silence.* JANET *laughs.*)

Something special you wanted to talk about?

AMY. A . . . you have very pretty hair.

JANET. Why, thank you, Amy.

AMY. Do you touch it up?

JANET. Oh, goodness, yes. It's really sort of dish-water. Although— so long since I've seen it, for all I know, it may be grey by now.

AMY. Oh? Frank's only twenty-seven.

JANET (*when she can catch her breath*). So many men are, at one time or another.

AMY. What do you mean?

JANET. I expect I'm just trying to cover a pause in the conversation.

AMY. Oh. (*She sits down now, without guile.*) You're engaged to your boss, aren't you?

JANET. Yes, I am.

AMY. Oughtn't you to spend some time with him?

JANET. He's in Toronto.

AMY. For much longer?

JANET. Two weeks longer.

AMY. Oh.
> (*The conversation languishes.* JANET *touches a petal of* AMY'S *skirt.*)

JANET. Your costume's awfully cute.

AMY. I think it's all wrong.

JANET. Well, a little torn perhaps.

AMY. I mean, you being engaged to a man far away, and seeing so much of Frank.

JANET. Oh, I don't see Frank that much. And besides—

AMY. You have lunch together every day, he told me so. And you've been over here to see him I don't know how many times.

JANET. But it's you I come to see too, Amy, and—

AMY. But I'm not talking about me. Frank just mustn't get tangled up with another man's girl.

JANET (*laughing*). We're not tangled up!

AMY. Oh, Frank isn't, I know.

JANET. But I am? Oh, come now!

AMY. Well, for your sake, I hope not. Because it could never work out. Frank's finally settled down.

JANET (*beginning to feel the strain*). Dear, I got your point! (*She rises and gets a cigarette.*)

AMY. I'm just trying to help you before you get in too deep.

JANET. Amy, look . . . Frank and I have a lot of fun together, but what I want now is something that will last. Security. Home of my own. And Frank can't offer that to anyone yet.

AMY. Then why keep hanging around him all the time?

JANET (*sharply*). Amy—now listen! Enough is enough. I told you—

AMY. Yes, but even you don't believe that now, do you?

JANET (*meets her eyes, suddenly turns away*). Yes, I do.

AMY. Frank always holds you up as being so blunt and honest! But you're not being honest now, or you'd have to admit you've fallen in love with him.

JANET. I—I have not.

AMY. You're not fooling me, Janet! I know what's in your heart.

JANET. You certainly do not!

AMY. I can see into your heart like it was my own! Because I know what Frank can do to a person. He's so beautiful and fine that just to be near him, you got to fall in love with him. Even if you don't want to, you can't help yourself. Before you can think, you're in love and it's too late.

(JANET *has turned and is staring at her, paralysed by* AMY's *impassioned self-betrayal.*)

JANET. How late is it, Amy?

AMY. So you'll think over what I said, won't you? Before it goes any farther?

JANET. Amy, please listen to me.

AMY There isn't time now, Frank'll be right down. And. if you wanted to go now, I could tell him you were tired. (*She opens the front door.*) Please, Janet. It's for your own good. You understand, don't you?

JANET (*heartsick*). Yes. I think I do.

AMY. Then hurry. Please.

(*But* FRANK *is already coming down the stairs.*)

FRANK. Well, we still got a party here?

AMY. No. I'm tired now. And Janet was just leaving.

FRANK (*to* JANET). Aw, not yet.

AMY. She wants to, Frank.

JANET. But . . . a . . . why not walk me out to the car, Amy? Finish
our talk.

AMY. I've said all there was. No, I'll say good-bye now. (*She starts
turning off the lights.*)

JANET (*urgently*). Then tomorrow? Let me come see you. Please.

FRANK (*mystified*). Hey, what's the pitch?

AMY. It's nothing. (*Going upstairs.*) I'll leave the hall light on for you.
You're coming right up, aren't you? (*He looks at* JANET.) Frank?

    (JANET *indicates that she wants to see him, and starts for the
front door.*)

FRANK. In a while. (*He follows* JANET.)

AMY. Where are you going?

FRANK. Out to the car with Janet.

AMY. No, it's late.

FRANK. So it's late.

AMY. Then you ought to be sleeping, you've a job to keep.

FRANK. I'll keep it okay! Now go up to bed!

AMY. Yes, get me out of the way! So she can stay!

FRANK. Amy, damn it—

AMY (*to* JANET). Oh, why didn't you go when I said?

FRANK. You shut up!

AMY. I'm tired of shutting up! And tired of strangers meddling!

JANET (*going to the door*). I'll phone you tomorrow, Frank.

FRANK (*to* AMY). You tell her you're sorry, and mighty damn quick!

JANET. Who would that help? Apologies don't cure things. They
just hide 'em a little longer.

    (*She goes out. The stair-lights flick on and* MRS. KITTRIDGE
appears at the head of the stairs in her bath-robe.)

FRANK. Janet, wait—

MRS. KITTRIDGE. Now, I've just had enough of this racket!

AMY (*obstructing him*). Let her go! We don't need her!

MRS. KITTRIDGE. Children!

FRANK (*to* AMY). You wait here! I've got something to tell you!
(*He heads for the door again.*)

MRS. KITTRIDGE. Where are you going, Frank?

(*But he is already on the front porch.*)

FRANK (*calling outside*). Janet! Hey, Janet!

MRS. KITTRIDGE. All this noise down here! What is it?

AMY. Nothing. (*But she looks about in panic for an escape.*)

MRS. KITTRIDGE. Well, I think you might have some consideration for your sisters and me. We live in this house, too.

(FRANK *comes in again, grimly.*)

FRANK. Amy—

MRS. KITTRIDGE. No! I don't want any more of this! Now come to bed! Right now! I don't want to come down and tell you children again! (*She returns upstairs, and the stair-lights flick off.*)

FRANK. What in hell's the matter with you?

AMY. Mama said there was too much noise.

FRANK. Noise be damned! Shaming me like that! What in hell you trying to do? Cut me off from the few friends I got?

AMY. If you think she's a friend, you're crazy!

FRANK. Not crazy enough so you're going to keep me here in solitary confinement! Next time I bring her around, you're going to behave, y'hear?

AMY. I won't! I hate her!

FRANK. Oh, for God's sake! Why?

AMY. She's a trouble maker! And dishonest!

FRANK. Oh, come on!

AMY. She is! Two-timing even her fiancé and pretending she's not. And I told her so!

FRANK. Amy, now damn it, you leave her alone! This is none of your business!

AMY. It is! That kind of woman would take any man she could get!

FRANK. I wish she'd just give me the chance!

AMY. Don't say that!

FRANK. I'm telling you, I wish she'd give me one chance!

(*In fury,* AMY *whirls on him, fists upraised. He catches her by the wrists, holding her momentarily helpless. Sinking her teeth into his hand,* AMY *wrests herself free, overturning a chair as she does.*)

AMY. All right, then! I wish you would leave us now!

FRANK. I'm not leaving anywhere for anyone! I said I'd stay here till you could shift for yourself. But I'll tell you this . . . you queer me with my friends again and, lady, I leave this house so damn fast you'll take me for lightning! Now get to bed! I'm sick of seeing you around!

AMY. No, Frank, wait . . . I didn't mean to. . . . Oh, won't you try and see? (*She has been been fighting against tears, but now they come.*) I'm desperate, don't you see? I don't know what to do any more.

> (*He has moved away uncomfortably from her tears. Now, with a sigh, he returns, takes her by the shoulders.*)

FRANK. Look—we'll talk it over tomorrow when you're calm. Now run on up and get some sleep.

> (*The stair-lights flick on, but they don't notice. MRS. KITTRIDGE's shadow then appears on the wall of the stairwell.*)

AMY. I couldn't sleep till I know for sure. That you don't hate me now.

FRANK. Why would I waste my time here if I hated you?

AMY. I didn't mean to make you trouble. It's only because I love you so much.

FRANK (*touched*). I love you too, honey.

AMY. As much as I love you?

FRANK. Twice as much. Now run on to bed.

> (*MRS. KITTRIDGE starts downstairs, smiling, but leaning forward to hear.*)

Say good night.

> (*He kisses AMY's cheek.*)

Okay?

> (*Suddenly AMY grips her arms around him and crushes her lips against his mouth. Almost convulsively, he flings her back. For an instant, stunned, half-crouching, they stare at each other. Scarcely audible.*)

FRANK. Why'd you do that?

AMY. I—I love you.

FRANK. Oh, no, Amy—you—don't know what you're saying.

AMY. I don't care! I love you.

FRANK. No, no, listen—

MRS. KITTRIDGE. Amy!

> (*FRANK and AMY turn. A moment of paralysed silence.*)

FRANK. Mama—

AMY. Mama, listen—

MRS. KITTRIDGE (*drawing back*). You—you couldn't. No!

FRANK. Go upstairs, Mama. You'll only make it worse.

Mrs. Kittridge (*calling*). Swart.

   (*Wheeling around,* Frank *strides out the front door.*)

Amy. Frank.

   (*She runs after him. The door bangs in her face. Confused and frightened,* Mrs. Kittridge *is staring at her, but* Amy *cannot face her. With a sob, she sinks to her knees.*)

I can't help it, Mama. I got to love someone.

Curtain

ACT THREE

Later that night. The clock has been striking. Mrs. Kittridge *is sitting in the dimly lit room, staring into nothingness.* Swart *comes from the dining-room with a cup and saucer.*

Swart. Mama . . .? Drink this. It'll help. Nice cup of hot coffee.

Mrs. Kittridge. Just—let me be.

Swart. Your hands are cold. Oh, come to bed now, Mama. You've been down here for hours. Please.

Mrs. Kittridge. Where's. . . . Is Amy . . .?

Swart. She's still in her room. But she won't open the door.

Mrs. Kittridge (*burying her face*). I—I don't—just don't know what to do.

Swart. If you'd only tell me what happened. It'd help to get it off your chest.

Mrs. Kittridge. I just—I can't discuss it.

Swart (*bitterly*). No. Not with me, apparently. But you'll probably confide in Frank all right!

(Mrs. Kittridge *draws back in dread.*)

Or—does he already know?

Mrs. Kittridge. No! We won't talk about it, not even think of it!

Swart. Mama, I don't want to say this, but I've got to—

Mrs. Kittridge. Swart! Oh, go back to bed, dear, forget I ever called you.

Swart. All right, Mama. (*She goes to front door and locks it.*)

Mrs. Kittridge. Why are you locking the door?

Swart. You said you didn't want to talk. But when Frank comes back, he'll make you talk, all right, all right.

Mrs. Kittridge. But—but he won't want to.

Swart. Won't he?

(*The stairway light turns on, and both turn quickly.* Amy *comes downstairs. Pale, tense, she is dressed and carries a shopping bag.* Mrs. Kittridge *draws back, cautioning* Swart.)

Mrs. Kittridge. I can't—I'm not ready to see her.

(*Upon seeing her mother,* Amy *freezes.*)

SWART. Dear, you better go back to your room.
> (AMY *takes another step down.*)

Do you hear me, Amy?
> (*Still* AMY *descends slowly.* SWART *tugs* MRS. KITTRIDGE'S
> *sleeve.*)

Mama?

MRS. KITTRIDGE (*with effort, summoning poise. To* AMY). Yes, it's—
very late and—better get some rest now. (AMY *hesitates, then continues down.*) Why don't you listen? I don't want— What—what's
that shopping bag?
> (AMY *hides it behind her.* SWART *grabs it and looks in.*)

AMY. It's nothing!

SWART. Your best clothes nothing?

MRS. KITTRIDGE. Your— What for?

AMY. Because I got to! Just for a few days. Hide away.

SWART (*bewildered*). What?

MRS. KITTRIDGE (*desperate to get* SWART *out of hearing*). Get her some
coffee, Swart. Some black coffee.

SWART. But Mama, can't I—

MRS. KITTRIDGE. At once! At once! (SWART *goes.* MRS. KITTRIDGE
turns back to AMY.) What do you mean, hide?

AMY. Where I could be by myself. There's no place here. Suddenly
no door I can lock.

MRS. KITTRIDGE. Now baby dear—now Amy.

AMY. Well, it's that or jump out the window!

MRS. KITTRIDGE. Amy!

AMY. I know. I know. That's no way out. Just childish. But I got
to do something. I'm so ashamed.

MRS. KITTRIDGE (*taking* AMY *in her arms*). There, there, there. It's
going to be all right now.

AMY. How can it, when—

MRS. KITTRIDGE. No, listen, dear—listen, listen. If you're sorry,
that's enough. Leave the rest to me.

AMY. Except you don't understand.

MRS. KITTRIDGE. I do, I do. Let Mama handle this and in a few days
there won't be a trace of it. Like someone had thrown a rock into a
lake, a beautiful lake. Now the surface is all disturbed and rough.
But the rock sinks out of sight, and soon the surface is calm again—
beautiful—just like it always was before. (*She tips up* AMY's *face.*)
Isn't that what we want?

AMY. More than anything. But—does Frank?

MRS. KITTRIDGE. Of course. He knows it was all a mistake.

AMY. Oh, Mama, you didn't see his face.

MRS. KITTRIDGE. How could I see anything when I was so sleepy?
So sleepy I almost wonder if I didn't dream the whole thing.

AMY. It's no use, Mama. He wouldn't let us.

> (*She starts for the side door again.* SWART *enters wtih some
> coffee.*)

MRS. KITTRIDGE. No, baby dear. Just let Mama think for you. That's
so much easier than running off alone and unprotected.

AMY. Don't make it harder for me, Mama. I don't want to go, but—
I just can't face Frank! (*She picks up her shopping bag.*)

SWART. Amy, wait.

> (*But* AMY *hurries out, side door.* SWART *follows.*)

Amy! Do you want to kill her?

> (*This stops* AMY. *She turns.*)

Then wait. Let me talk to her. I can fix things.

> (*She takes the shopping bag from* AMY *and hastens back inside.*)

Now listen, Mama—you heard what Amy said; she can't face
Frank!

> (MRS. KITTRIDGE *tries to interrupt.*)

I don't know what happened tonight, but I do know she'll leave the
home she loves rather than see him again.

MRS. KITTRIDGE. Oh, no, no!

SWART. There's no way you can stop her. Unless you send Frank
packing.

MRS. KITTRIDGE. Send— No! I won't break up my family. Not
again!

SWART. You've no choice any more. Amy will go if Frank doesn't.

MRS. KITTRIDGE. I tell you, I'll be able to—

SWART. Amy or Frank, Mama! Which'll it be?

MRS. KITTRIDGE (*frantically*). No. Later I'll find a way later, if you just
give me time!

> (*Someone tries to open the front door, startling both. They turn
> to the door.* MRS. KITTRIDGE *whispers.*)

Is it Frank?

> (*A knock on the door.* MRS. KITTRIDGE *starts toward it.* SWART
> *grasps her by the arm and draws her back.*)

SWART. Come with me. Please, Mama. You know he's not wanted
here any more.

FRANK (*calling outside*). Mama? Let me in, will you?

        (MRS. KITTRIDGE *turns again to the door.*)

SWART. Please, Mama.

MRS. KITTRIDGE (*frantically*). I can manage him. He loves me, he'll want to do what I say.

SWART. All right then! But by tomorrow morning, Amy will have left home. And we'll all know why!

MRS. KITTRIDGE (*for the first time jolted into alertness*). What?

SWART. Yes! You're trying to shield me from something. But Frank won't. He'll use it like a weapon. If that's what you want, let him in! (*She rushes upstairs.*)

MRS. KITTRIDGE. No, Swart, wait—Swart!

FRANK (*outside*). Mama? The door's locked.

MRS. KITTRIDGE. Swart—don't leave me alone. Swart!

        (FRANK *hammers at the door. She looks at the door and then at the stairs, locked by conflict, wholly unable to act.*)

FRANK. Mama, if you don't open this door, I'm smashing it in. Now I'm going to count three. One—

MRS. KITTRIDGE. Wait, I'm coming, I'm coming.

        (*Hurriedly, she undoes the chains and unlocks the door.* FRANK *enters, followed by* JANET.)

FRANK. What took you so long?

MRS. KITTRIDGE. I—I was upstairs, I didn't hear.

FRANK. Where's Amy?

MRS. KITTRIDGE. Amy? She—she's asleep. It's nearly morning, for heaven's sake!

        (FRANK *looks at his watch, then at* JANET *questioningly.*)

FRANK. What do you think?

JANET. The sooner the better, Frank.

MRS. KITTRIDGE (*frantically attempting charm*). And you should be asleep, too. Right now, you bad boy. Where've you been all this time?

FRANK. Mama, you want to ask Amy to come down?

MRS. KITTRIDGE. Dear, Mama asked you a question.

JANET. We drove to New London, Mrs. Kittridge.

MRS. KITTRIDGE (*uneasily*). What for?

FRANK. Amy has a friend there. Doc Hawkins. We wanted to talk to him.

MRS. KITTRIDGE. That horse doctor? What . . . what could you talk

to him about? Not—you didn't discuss— Not in front of strangers!
(*And now she looks at* JANET *in dread.*) With her, too?
FRANK. Aw, Mama! I asked you to get Amy. Won't you please do
it?

(MRS. KITTRIDGE *inches back towards porch door.*)

Well?
MRS. KITTRIDGE. Leave her alone, Frank. Don't make any trouble.
FRANK. I'm not going to make it, I want to fix it.
MRS. KITTRIDGE. There's no need to now. She already knows she
made a mistake. That's enough.
FRANK. That's only the beginning, Mother. We need to help her now.
(*He starts for stairs.*)
MRS. KITTRIDGE (*drawing him back*). What kind of help could you give
her when you're so wrought up? If you try to talk to her now, that
child will leave us!
FRANK. That's right. Probably will.
MRS. KITTRIDGE. Now? When she needs her family as never before?
No, darling, no. She's already so frightened, she talked of doing
away with herself. You've got to let me handle this. I can. I have
before.
FRANK. Yeah, I know how you handled it before. Protected her from
everything!
MRS. KITTRIDGE. It carried her through disaster, didn't it? And it will
again!
FRANK. Will you listen? Amy fell in love with me! Fell in love with
her own brother! (*Wincing,* MRS. KITTRIDGE *whispers* "Hush!")
Now, damn it, are you just going to ignore it.
MRS. KITTRIDGE. No! But I'll take her responsibility.
FRANK. You don't have the right to!
MRS. KITTRIDGE. Love gives me the right!
FRANK. Shielding Amy from her own responsibility isn't love! That's
fear! And it has no right!
MRS. KITTRIDGE. Then you don't understand what love is!
FRANK. Well, stick around! Because me and Amy are going to have
quite a talk about what love is! (*He starts for the stairs.*)
MRS. KITTRIDGE (*following*). I forbid you to! I'm still the mother in
this house, and we'll do as I say! (FRANK *continues up the stairs.*)
She's not up there, Frank! (*He turns in surprise.*) On my word of
honour.
FRANK (*returning to her*). Then where is she, Mother?

T.S.–E

MRS. KITTRIDGE. I—I don't know.

FRANK. Where!

MRS. KITTRIDGE. Oh, don't make me sorry you ever came back to me!

JANET. Frank, it's not doing any good like this.

MRS. KITTRIDGE. Amy's not in this house. Ran off to the neighbours hours ago. Now leave her alone!

(*Again she has edged toward the side door.* FRANK, *suddenly motionless, narrows his gaze at her.*)

What?

FRANK (*indicating the side door*). Why do you keep crowding that door?

MRS. KITTRIDGE. I don't.

FRANK (*coming toward her*). I'll take a look.

MRS. KITTRIDGE. No, she's not out there!

FRANK. On the porch? In the stable?

(*On the porch,* AMY *inches back into the shadows.*)

MRS. KITTRIDGE. She's not there, I tell you!

FRANK. Then call her. If she's not there it won't make any difference. Call her!

MRS. KITTRIDGE. No!

(*That's all the proof he needs; he starts for the door again. Spreading her arms, she backs against the door so he cannot pass.*)

I'm warning you.

FRANK. Get out of my way, Mama!

(MRS. KITTRIDGE *presses more tightly against the door. As he reaches around in back of her for the door knob, she slaps his face sharply.*)

MRS. KITTRIDGE. You get out of my house! (*A silence, as her own words ring back in her ears. Aghast, but adamant, she meets his eyes fiercely.*) I never thought I'd be saying that. Closed my ears and eyes to everyone who warned me against you. Even when I knew they were right, I wouldn't listen. No—instead, I made sacrifices, I made changes. Opened my house to strangers. Even opened my heart to your girl. But all the time I've been trying to keep us together, you've been trying to break us up. Well, if it makes you happy, you nearly have! Nearly destroyed all of us! But you're not going to any more. (*Looking away, as if from some impertinent stranger.*) As soon as you collect your gear, I want you out of this house!

FRANK. First thing I'm collecting is Amy. So if you'll get away from that door—

> (MRS. KITTRIDGE *does not move.*)

I don't want to hurt you, Mother.

MRS. KITTRIDGE. You've done very well, already!

> (*Grasping her by the shoulders, he forcibly pushes her aside. Outside, on the porch,* AMY *rushes out into the dark garden.* FRANK *bursts out on to the empty porch.* JANET *hastens after him.*)

JANET. Frank! Frank, wait!

MRS. KITTRIDGE (*following*). She's not out here! I told you she wasn't!

> (*He starts to go into the garden.* JANET *draws him back.*)

JANET. She's frightened of you now, Frank. Even if you do find her, she won't listen to you!

> (*He stops, knowing she is right. Then he looks out into the garden and calls.*)

FRANK. Amy.

MRS. KITTRIDGE. No! Be still!

FRANK. Amy, if you can hear me—don't be afraid. I know you're near.

MRS. KITTRIDGE. She's not even out there, I tell you!

FRANK. Listen, Amy, I—I drove out and saw Doc Hawkins tonight, and—he needs an assistant. Amy, I could drive you out to see him right now, if you wanted—get you settled there.

MRS. KITTRIDGE. And then abandon her? Is that how you plan to punish her?

FRANK. It's not to punish, Amy!

MRS. KITTRIDGE. No? Leaving her out there when she's had no experience being on her own? It's not even easy for people like you. Yes! It's sink or swim out there, and even you went under. So what chance would poor Amy have?

FRANK. She's right about that, Amy. It's sink or swim. But you learned to swim before. Our day at the beach, remember? Oh, honey, you want to swim in that sea! Not just listen to it in a seashell. (*Desperately holding out his arms to the darkness.*) Oh, come on in, Amy! The water's fine!

> (*He searches the darkness, listening for some sign.* SWART *appears at the top of the stairs, uneasily. Again* FRANK *calls.*)

Amy!

MRS. KITTRIDGE. Where is she, Frank? She can hear you, I'm sure. Then why doesn't she come back? The answer must be clear even to you. She doesn't want to see you. Doesn't want to talk to you. (*She starts back inside.*) I tried to tell you that, but you wouldn't believe. However, if you still don't believe me, call her again.

(*She goes inside. Quickly,* SWART *comes down the stairs to her.*)

Call her. It won't do any good.

(FRANK *and* JANET *trade glances. Then he calls once more.*)

FRANK. Amy—please, honey.

(*Again he listens. There is only silence. With a sigh, he goes inside.* JANET *follows.*)

JANET. Give her a little time to think. Then tomorrow when she's calm, try again.

MRS. KITTRIDGE. I'm afraid not.

(*They turn to her.*)

Frank will be leaving now. (*Turning to* SWART.) His stuff is in the cellar, if you'll fetch it now, Swart.

(SWART *goes into the dining-room.* MRS. KITTRIDGE *starts for the side door, but even now, an impossible longing to forgive makes her way difficult. Faltering, she clings to an arm-chair for support. She touches its cushion as if for comfort, and there are tears in her eyes and a terrible smile on her lips.*)

When you were a baby you spilled ink on this chair.

(*The tears threaten to get out of control and murmuring "Oh, Frank", she hastens out on to the side porch; leans against a pilaster, hiding her face. After a moment,* AMY *comes out of the garden on to the porch and, putting her arms around her mother, comforts her. With a gasp of relief,* MRS. KITTRIDGE *clings to her.*)

There, there, you'll be all right now. I promise, I promise.

FRANK (*indoors, bitterly quiet*). Aw, the hell with it all.

(*He goes to the stair closet, begins flinging out some of his clothes.*)

JANET. I think there's a vacancy at my place.

FRANK (*sick of it. Almost toneless*). I'm not staying around here. God, no.

JANET. Where then?

FRANK. What's the difference? Any place the road leads to, long as it takes me far enough away.

JANET. Got any money to get there? (*He looks at her sharply.*) I've got about ten bucks—(*Opens her purse.*)—but remember, it's just a loan!

(*This snaps him out of it. He has to smile, however wearily.*)

FRANK. You make me feel like such a— (*He goes to her, takes her in his arms.*) Look—I don't know if I still got any prospects in Portland, but—would you want to come there with me?

JANET. You mean—right now? (FRANK *nods. A bit ruefully, she presses her cheek to his shoulder.*) That'd certainly be the easy way, wouldn't it? Not thinking twice. Just rushing off with a bang and a kiss and a clatter. But—

FRANK. But—

JANET. Oh, Frank, I didn't even admit to myself what I felt about you till tonight, and—even yet, I'm not sure it's love.

FRANK. We want each other. That's enough.

JANET. Enough for how long? (*He is silent.*) It's not the answer.

FRANK. But marrying your boss you don't love, is?

JANET. No, that's not the answer either. I don't have any answers any more. They all kind of fell to pieces tonight, and I haven't had time since to think out what I really do want out of life. Time to face up to myself, for once. Time, even, to—to see if I'll miss you when you're gone.

FRANK. Then—you're staying? (*She nods. He sighs and laughs wryly.*) Looks like I'm leavin' this house without accomplishing a bloody thing!

(DERST *comes downstairs, buttoning her dress.*)

DERST. Aren't you ever going to bed? (FRANK'S *and* JANET'S *eyes meet. They smile ruefully and step apart. Glimpsing* JANET *now,* DERST *is mortified.*) Oh, I—I didn't mean— Well, not like it sounded. I— I—(*She sighs and gives it up.*)

(SWART *returns with duffle bag and some heavy shoes, dumping them on the floor.*)

SWART. No trouble. No trouble at all!

JANET (*crossing to the front door*). I'll wait outside in the car for you, Frank. (*She goes.*)

SWART (*seeing* DERST. *Uncomfortably*). What are you doing up?

DERST. There was so much noise going on down here, I thought it was morning.

(FRANK *picks up his gear and, a bit forlornly, starts upstairs. As he passes* DERST, *she pats his shoulder, and for a moment he presses his cheek against her hand. Then he continues upstairs.*)

DERST. What's he doing with his duffle bag? Going somewhere? (*She has said this jokingly, but* SWART *nods far too seriously.*) Oh, you're fooling! Why, we'd die of boredom if he left. (SWART *only shrugs and looks away.*) Are you serious? He's really leaving?

SWART. Yes.

DERST. But—why?

SWART. Because.

DERST. Because why?

SWART. I don't know.

DERST. Where's Mama?

SWART. On the side porch. Don't bother her now.

DERST (*heading for porch, calling*). Oh, Mama.

SWART. No, Derst! She's all worn out!

DERST (*opening side door*). Mama!

MRS. KITTRIDGE. No, ask Swart to help you. I just can't cope with anything more tonight.

DERST. But Mama, I just saw Frank, and—

MRS. KITTRIDGE (*to* AMY). I'll be right back, baby dear, don't you worry. (*Coming into the parlour, closing the door. Anxiously.*) What's this about Frank? What did he tell you?

DERST. Nothing, but—he had his duffle bag and— Why is he leaving us?

MRS. KITTRIDGE. What?

DERST. Why is he going?

(MRS. KITTRIDGE *turns away in confusion.*)

Mama?

MRS. KITTRIDGE. I—I don't know why.

DERST. But you must!

MRS. KITTRIDGE (*fiercely*). I—I can't go on talk-talk-talking about this the rest of my life! There's got to be an end to it somewhere! It's got to be forgotten! Now, be still! Be still!

(DERST *looks at her, hurt and astonished. Suddenly, she runs to the stairs.*)

Where are you going?

DERST. To ask Frank.

MRS. KITTRIDGE. No! I forbid you!

(*On the porch,* AMY *rises and comes to the door.*)

DERST. Well, someone's got to tell me. And if you won't—

MRS. KITTRIDGE. But how can I tell you when he has no reason? Men don't need a reason, they just suddenly desert you. Your father did the same.

(*Unnoticed,* AMY *has opened the side door.*)

DERST. But it's not the same! Father left us for some woman.

(*The last word scarcely gets out of her mouth when a similar answer comes to all of them.*

They stand seized by silence, exchanging glances of apprehension.)
What do you mean?
(*But no one speaks. Picking up the coat* JANET *left on the sofa,* DERST *glances up the stairs, then at her mother.*)
Is that it? Frank too? Like our father did?
(*Even yet* MRS. KITTRIDGE *is reluctant to use this device.*)
For Janet? Frank's deserting us for her?
MRS. KITTRIDGE (*quietly at last*). What other reason could there be?
DERST. Oh, no! If I beg them to stay—if I ask Janet, she always liked me. (*She starts for the front door.*)
MRS. KITTRIDGE. Derst!
(DERST *falters, then turns back,* MRS. KITTRIDGE *puts her arms around her.*)
There's nothing that can be done now. Nothing. Now—you forced me to tell you girls, but from here on, I don't want it even whispered about. Ever! Is that understood? We'll have to do just like we did when your father deserted us: we didn't discuss it, and after a while—we forgot!
(DERST *turns away to hide her tears.*)
Now, I—I think the best things you girls can do is—go to your rooms and—
(SWART *sees* AMY *in the side doorway and warns her mother.*)
SWART. Amy.
(MRS. KITTRIDGE *turns. For a long moment, she and* AMY *look at each other. Then, asking* AMY's *confederacy with a nervous signal,* MRS. KITTRIDGE *goes on.*)
MRS. KITTRIDGE. Go to your rooms and close the doors. Just till Frank leaves the house. Right now. All of you.
SWART. Come along, Derst. (*She starts upstairs.*) Get something to read.
DERST. Yes—something to read. (*She goes to the closet where her magazines are stored.*)
AMY. Mama?
MRS. KITTRIDGE. No, I'll—(*To avoid further discussion, she hastens into the dining-room.*)—I'll bring you up some warm milk.
(*She goes out. Slowly,* AMY *starts upstairs.*)
DERST. Something to read. (*Glances blindly at one of her magazines. Suddenly.*) Something to read!

(*She fires it across the room. Then flings another and another until their flapping pages seem to fill the room like frightened pigeons.*)

AMY (*turning at the landing*). What are you— Derst! Derst!

(*She comes running downstairs. To escape questions and to hide her tears,* DERST *quickly opens a movie magazine and pretends to be reading.*)

What is it?

DERST (*holding up the magazine*). Look—Bette Davis.

(SWART *reappears on the stairs.*)

SWART. Derst, aren't you coming— (*And then seeing the disarray, hurries down anxiously.*) Dearest?

DERST (*glibly*). I always loved her most of all, Bette Davis. That movie where she was the rich titled lady and he was a devil-may-care playboy and . . . and—

(*Her ruse fails, and she breaks down.* AMY *tries to help her to the sofa.*)

Nothing. It's nothing.

AMY. Because of—what Mama just told you?

DERST. About Frank? (*She nods tearfully.*)

AMY. I—I'm sorry, Derst.

DERST. It's not your fault.

SWART (*gently*). Dear, she said not to talk about it any more.

AMY (*to* DERST). Does this change everything?

DERST. Oh, I wish it would! Mama said it'd all be like it was before. But I can't go back to that! (*With fresh grief.*) At least Frank made it seem like the world was still exciting and I was part of it. But now —to sink back again to the dark room—nothing to hope for, trying to forget all I missed, pretending I don't mind, pretending I'm happy.

SWART. Oh, Derst, that's not true!

DERST. It's true of us all! All of us! At least Mama has her children and garden to help her pretend she still matters. But I don't have anything. Because I can't go back to just movie magazines. I've read 'em all ten million times. I know every line—what size shoe Bette Davis wears and who she went dancing with. I know all about her, and she doesn't even know I'm alive. Well—I'm not alive. And now there's no way left to pretend I am!

AMY. Oh, Derst, I—I'll make up to you for it. That's the only reason I'm staying here now. To make up for everything. Oh, trust me!

DERST. Yes, Frank said that, too, and I did trust him. But I won't any more. And I'll never forgive him either!

SWART. Dearest, we're not supposed to talk about it. Please come along.

DERST (*rising*). Well, let him run out on us then! If that's all he thinks of us, good riddance!

AMY. That's not fair to say! Maybe—maybe he thought he was doing the right thing, the best thing.

SWART. Deserting us for that blonde, the right thing?

DERST. You don't have to smooth things over, Amy. That's Mama's way.

AMY. But what I mean is—for all we know, Janet may not be the real reason at all.

DERST. Mama wouldn't lie about it.

AMY. Unless ... (*She hesitates.*) I ... don't know. (*They start upstairs again. She forces herself to speak again.*) Unless.—

DERST. What is it, dear?

AMY. Oh, Derst—there are so many things in the heart that—that you can't explain because—because you— What I mean is— is—

SWART. Whatever you're trying to say, dear, say it!

AMY (*turning away in despair*). I can't! No, it's ... it's nothing.

SWART. Then—you were just covering up for Frank and Janet.

(MRS. KITTRIDE *comes in with a glass of milk. Seeing her daughters together startles her.*)

MRS. KITTRIDGE. I thought I told you girls to go to your rooms.

SWART. We were just going. (*She and* DERST *start.*)

MRS. KITTRIDGE (*uneasily*). I hope you haven't been talking about— (*Their faces tell her they have been talking.*) Now I asked you not to!

AMY. I didn't say anything. But, Mama, it's not fair!

(DERST *and* SWART *pause on stairs.* MRS. KITTRIDGE, *aware of their confusion now, puts an arm around* AMY.)

MRS. KITTRIDGE. No, dear, it's not fair—Frank, deserting us that way. Not fair at all. But you'll get used to it. Tomorrow, it'll be easier. And the day after, easier still. Now—come along. Let's go back to sleep. All of us. (*She shepherds* DERST *and* SWART *along the stairs.*) Up to beddie-byes.

(AMY *has not yet moved.*)

Baby dear?

(*With a sigh,* AMY *starts for the stairs.* SWART, *who has gone upstairs, quickly reappears. In a whisper.*)

SWART. He's coming down.

                    (AMY *inches back in alarm.*)

MRS. KITTRIDGE. We can just wait in the dining-room.

FRANK (*coming downstairs*). Don't bother. It's all yours.

      (*He crosses the room.* DERST *and* SWART *turn their backs on him.*
MRS. KITTRIDGE *starts for dining-room but* AMY, *paralysed with self-consciousness, does not move.*

      Not looking at her, FRANK *takes some keys and a coin from his pocket, drops them on the desk.*)

Here are my door keys. And fifty cents I owe the newspaper boy. And—when Doc Hawkins phones, tell him I'm sorry I got his hopes up.

      (*He picks up the seashell and looks at it for a moment. Then unties the knot in his duffle bag. Still not looking at* AMY.)

Good-bye, Amy. Guess you know now why Dad wanted to get us away from here when we were kids.

MRS. KITTRIDGE. Come along, baby.

      (*He takes a shirt from duffle bag and carefully wraps the sea-shell in it.*)

FRANK. To save us from just this kind of life. Mama's way of life.

MRS. KITTRIDGE (*uneasily*). That's not why he left. It was for some woman.

FRANK. There was no woman. I'd know, wouldn't I? I was with Dad. There never was any woman, and Mama knows it. She just dreamed up that story because it was less painful than blaming herself. And that's her way of life in a nutshell.

      (*Finishing wrapping the shell, he stuffs it into the full duffle bag and starts tying its drawstrings.*)

MRS. KITTRIDGE. I'm going upstairs now, Amy dear.

FRANK. Changing the facts or hiding 'em, so she'll never have to face anything painful. Even if it gets worse.

      (*He heads for the door. His words have had special meaning for* AMY, *however, and she looks at her mother searchingly.* MRS. KITT-RIDGE *sees this and grasps her arm.*)

MRS. KITTRIDGE. Your father did desert me for some woman!

AMY. Did he, Mama?

MRS. KITTRIDGE. Yes!

AMY. Like Frank?

(*He has opened the front door to go, but now turns back in surprise.*)

MRS. KITTRIDGE (*uneasily*). Hush!

FRANK. What's this?

MRS. KITTRIDGE. Just come along now, and it'll be all right.

AMY. Shifting the blame on to Frank?

MRS. KITTRIDGE. Hush!

AMY. I don't want to be protected that way any more, Mama!

MRS. KITTRIDGE (*drawing her aside, sharply*). And I thought you were the girl who was so ashamed!

AMY (*wresting free*). I am ashamed! But I'd rather tell the truth now and be done with it, than hide from it all the rest of my life!

MRS. KITTRIDGE (*to* DERST *and* SWART). Come along.

(DERST *and* SWART *start to go upstairs.* AMY *takes a step after them, lifting her voice.*)

AMY. Frank's not leaving because of Janet! It's because of me!

(DERST *and* SWART *turn to look at her.*)

I was in love with him. That's why he had to leave!

MRS. KITTRIDGE (*her hands over her ears*). No! No!

AMY. I did! I loved him!

MRS. KITTRIDGE. Of course you loved him. I love him, too. So do all of us.

AMY. That's not the love I mean, and you know it!

(MRS. KITTRIDGE *turns and looks at her, then speaks deliberately.*)

MRS. KITTRIDGE. Well, I do know this: you don't love us.

AMY. I do, Mama! But—

MRS. KITTRIDGE. Then you won't force your sisters and me to believe any such wild story about you. (AMY *looks at her mother unbelievingly.*) Why, if we believed such a hideous thing, it'd haunt us for the rest of our lives, make it impossible for us to go on living together as a family.

AMY (*seeing the pattern too clearly now*). Mother!

MRS. KITTRIDGE. So tell your sisters you were only lying. Then they can forget.

DERST. Mama, maybe we'd better wait.

MRS. KITTRIDGE (*insistently, to* AMY). All your life we've protected you, and you owe us the same!

SWART (*anxiously taking her mother's arm*). It won't help now, Mama.

MRS. KITTRIDGE. The loving thing to do. Tell them it never happened.

(*Touching at* AMY *with blind-man's hands.*) It can't have happened. . . .
Please! Please.

> (AMY *looks at her dazedly, then slowly turns to* SWART; *but it is
> a moment before she can say it.*)

AMY.   Swart, I. . . . (*She hesitates, then kisses her.*) Goodbye, sweetheart.

> MRS. KITTRIDGE *looks at her uncomprehendingly.* AMY *crosses to*
> DERST.)

Good-bye, dearest.

MRS. KITTRIDGE. Amy!

DERST. But—where will you go?

AMY. To stay with Doc Hawkins. It's not too far if you—if you ever
want to come see me.

MRS. KITTRIDGE. Amy—Oh, no, you're not leaving!

> (*She kisses* DERST, *then crosses for her shopping bag.*)

Please, Amy, listen—listen.

SWART (*quietly*). Don't Mama.

MRS. KITTRIDGE (*following* AMY, *pleading*). It was for your own good.
I wouldn't have asked it if I hadn't loved you.

> (AMY *opens the front door.*)

Please, darling, don't you desert me, too.

> (AMY *turns at the door, looks at her mother without rancour, but
> without weakness either; it is something very like compassion.*)

AMY. Good-bye, Mother.

> (*She turns, pauses a moment more on the threshold, looking in
> wonderment at the grey light beginning to change the darkness. Then
> she goes.*)

MRS. KITTRIDGE (*scarcely more than a whisper*). Amy.

> (*She looks to* FRANK *now. He removes his cap and their eyes
> hold for a brief moment. Then he shoulders his duffle bag and goes,
> closing the door behind him.*)

Amy.

DERST (*gently*). Wait— (*She picks up her coat and starts for the door.*)

MRS. KITTRIDGE. What are you doing?

> (DERST *falters, then lowers her eyes.* MRS. KITTRIDGE *takes the
> coat away from her.*)

No sense in rushing around this way when—when Amy will be
right back. Why—probably tonight.

SWART. Oh, Mama! Even you don't believe that.

(MRS. KITTRIDGE *makes an enormous effort to hide her despair,
to get the old magic going again.*)

MRS. KITTRIDGE. I do! Yes—we'll get her room all ready. Come,
Swart.

SWART. I. . . . No. I—I can't, Mama. (*She turns and hastens upstairs.*)

MRS. KITTRIDGE. Then Derst will. Won't you, dear?

(*But* DERST *is gazing into a mirror and does not answer.*)

Dear?

(DERST *turns to her quietly.*)

What is it?

DERST. I was just wondering.

MRS. KITTRIDGE. Wondering what?

DERST. How I'd look if I blondined my hair some day, Mama.

(*Quietly, and with dignity, she goes into the dining-room.*)

MRS. KITTRIDGE. Derst?

(*But* DERST *does not answer.*)

Girls!

(*Bewildered, worn out, she looks around the empty room. Unable
to comprehend yet that she is alone, she calls, as she used to at twilight
when dinner was ready.*)

Children . . . children. . . .

THE CURTAIN IS FALLING.

PROPERTY LIST

PROPERTY LIST

Easy chair
Round table
Two chairs (for it)
Two small tables
Barometer
Bookshelves
Shelf (with ornaments)
Table lamps
Pictures
Curtains
Carpets
Flowers in vases
Chandelier
Flower-pot
Desk (bills on it)
Pincushion (loaded)
Purse (planted)
Seashell (packaged)
Birthday presents
Wrapping and string

Decorations
Magazines
Books
Sofa
Ouija board
Champagne glasses
Wall mirror

Off

Cookies and milk
Gift boxes
Plant in pot
Ginger ale
Cup and saucer

Effects

Telephone
Car horn
Door bell
Clock striking

PERSONAL

Shopping bag (Amy)
Keys and coins (Frank)
Shirt (in duffle-bag—Frank)
Roses and apples in basket (Mrs. Kittridge)
Harmonica ⎫
Glove ⎬ Mrs.
Roller skate ⎪ Kittridge
Movie magazines ⎭

Duffle-bag and packages (Frank)
Quills (Amy)
Watch (Swart)
Bathrobe (Swart)
Newspaper (Mrs. Kittridge)
Ring (Marietta)
Paper crown (Mrs. Kittridge)